$elf
PUBLISHED
MILLIONAIRE

The **Step-By-Step** Guide to Writing, Publishing and
Marketing Your First Book

JOSEPH ALEXANDER
& TIM PETTINGALE

www.self-published.co.uk

British Library Cataloguing in Publication Data
A catalogue record for this book is available from the British Library.

ISBN 978-1-78933-025-0

www.self-published.co.uk

Contents

Get the Supporting Media

This book tells the story of how a successful self-publishing enterprise was created from scratch, and gives the reader a clear strategy to follow, so that you can do the same. To prevent the book from becoming out of date, some of the step-by-step guides are provided to readers as free downloads from our website. These will be kept up to date as publishing methods change. There you will find detailed charts, templates, written guides and tuition videos to walk you through each step of the publishing process.

Visit **www.self-published.co.uk** for all the resources you need to make your self-publishing a huge success. Along with essential tools, you'll find interviews with other best-selling, self-published authors who share their stories. We also have a (non-spammy) mailing list you can sign up to and receive exclusive tips, tricks, and up to date insights about how the self-publishing industry is developing.

Get the free resources here:

http://geni.us/authordownloads
https://www.self-published.co.uk/resources-for-authors/

Twitter: @**spm_author**
Facebook: **https://www.facebook.com/groups/SPMauthor/**

Our new authors' Facebook group will be particularly useful for you to interact with others on a similar journey, get feedback and ask questions on any aspect of self-publishing. We're a friendly bunch, so join in now!

What This Book Will Teach You

In this book we will show you, step-by-step, how to take your idea and turn it into a professionally published book, able to compete in the busy online marketplace. Continuing where most self-publishing guides leave off, we will go beyond the mechanics of publishing and drill down into the detail of running a successful marketing campaign and building your audience.

We will give insights into how Joseph created the **www.fundamental-changes.com** brand and successfully self-published over 100 titles that have reached a global audience, selling more than 400,000 copies. Fundamental Changes publishes non-fiction, music tuition books, but the principles taught here can be applied to a wide range of other books. We will include examples and case studies from other types of non-fiction and fiction too – so no matter what you want to write, you'll find relevant advice.

We will teach you the whole process of planning, writing and publishing, from concept to completion, in clear, organised steps you can replicate for your genre. You may find that your rhythm for writing is slightly different to ours, but all of the tasks relating to cover design, marketing, gaining readers, formatting, outsourcing and publishing, apply to all self-published authors. We've broken down each part of the process, made it as straight forward as possible, and given you plenty of tips and tricks along the way.

When we say we are sharing our entire process for self-publishing success, we're not kidding! We are not holding back anything. From an insider's guide to publishing on Amazon, through to the email automation strategies we use to keep and attract new readers, everything is here. Depending on where you are in your self-publishing journey, you may wish to skip ahead to the chapters that focus on specific tasks and spend your time where you feel you'll gain the most benefit.

Finally, it's important to point out that while there are other methods of distribution for self-published authors, the focus of this book is achieving publishing success using Amazon's global online stores. We will, however, add guides on other methods to our website.

Getting started – what you should do right now

Sign up for all the essential content on **www.self-published.co.uk**

Register at **KDP.Amazon.com**. This is where you will publish and upload your paperback book to Amazon, and publish the digital edition of your book. If you already have an Amazon account, you use your same credentials to log in to KDP.

Register at: **https://advertising.amazon.co.uk/** This is where you will run advertising campaigns for your book, using Amazon's Advertising Console.

Join our Facebook Page and get chatting to other authors: **https://www.facebook.com/groups/SPMauthor/**

Follow us on Twitter for regular publishing tips: **@spm_author**

Sign up for **MailChimp** – the free (for up to 2,000 people) mailing list host you will use to develop the marketing of your books.

Joseph's Story

"Joseph Alexander is a one-man genre, dominating his category with great books and marketing excellence. The competition might as well pack up and go home."
Mark Dawson, USA Today Bestseller (over 2 million books sold)

"Joseph Alexander is a self-publishing phenomenon with a sharp eye for marketing and an even sharper eye for what makes a good book."
L.J. Ross, Bestselling Author (over 3 million books sold)

* * *

I really struggled at music college. I mean *really* struggled. I was probably the least talented guitarist in my year and found myself practising eight hours a day just to keep my head above water.

Going to a London music school was an honour and a privilege, but I couldn't keep up with the workload in such a competitive environment. Each week I was given music to learn by vastly different musicians and I struggled to process this information overload. I believed that I had to get all these influences into my playing instantly, when actually it would take years to fully master a small number of these skills. In fact, I was never taught to prioritise the most important musical ideas, so I tried to work on everything all at once. Unsurprisingly, my guitar playing sucked.

This overload led to me having a breakdown and quitting music college. I took a year off to get my head together and transferred to Leeds College of Music in the north of England. Leeds saved me as a musician and one conversation with my guitar teacher in particular sticks in my memory.

On my very first lesson, my teacher Jiannis asked me who I wanted to play like. Who was my biggest influence?

"Pat Martino," I said.

"OK. The way you're practising you're never going to get there," he told me. Jiannis held his hand high up by the ceiling and looked up at it.

"That's Martino, yeah? He's a god."

"Sure!"

Next Jiannis leant down, putting his hand an inch off the floor.

"This is you. Compared to him, you're shit. You'll never make it."

"Right…" I was almost in tears.

Jiannis stretched both arms out wide, struggling to show the distance between Martino and me.

"The reason you'll never make it is because you're trying to make this massive leap all in one go. You'll fail quickly, and you'll fail hard. You've already seen that."

"OK…"

"But, what you can do is this…" Jiannis used his thumb and index finger to measure out about half an inch.

"It's really easy to move a tiny step forward many times, but it is impossible to make the kind of leap you're aiming for in one go.

Everything suddenly clicked for me. A huge burden had been lifted. I was suddenly able to stop judging myself against world-class musicians and free to focus only on the next tiny, logical step in my playing.

It may seem obvious, but that short conversation changed me as a musician and as a person.

Over the next two years Jiannis fed me music in incremental steps, teaching me piece by piece the small individual skills I needed to master in order to play jazz. As I managed each tiny task, I received constant, positive reinforcement. I quickly learned that I could enjoy guitar again if I regularly accomplished small goals, rather than forever feeling trapped under the weight of my own unrealistic expectations.

It was my teacher's job to keep an eye on the big picture and my job to complete the tasks he assigned me each week. His one rule was that I worked *only* on his assignments and didn't get distracted by the multitude of other musical possibilities such as books, the Internet and other teachers, etc.

This rule of non-distraction was the second most important thing he taught me. It's also the reason I started writing and now receive $60,000 a month in royalties.

After music college, I found myself with a degree in Jazz and therefore completely unqualified to do anything that society would deem "useful"! Luckily for me, I always loved teaching guitar and after my struggles in London and my success in Leeds, it gave me a good livelihood.

Because I'd never been a natural talent at guitar, I had been forced to develop the ability to break down music into its most basic parts. I learned how to "reverse engineer" music so I could teach it to myself, piece by piece. This skill was instrumental in my teaching because I could break down skills and techniques and easily pass them on to my students.

After teaching hundreds of guitarists I noticed that many were approaching me with similar "overload" issues to those I'd experienced in London. This time, however, the problem was YouTube! There are so many resources available that my aspiring guitarists were confused as to what they should work on. With so many voices telling them what they "needed" to know, they sought my advice to help put everything into context.

Now it was my turn to hold my hand high up to the ceiling and separate my finger and thumb about an inch!

It occurred to me that as so many students were suffering with the same issues, particularly with regards to learning jazz, I should create hand-out sheets to save time in lessons. I sketched out a complete study-path for an aspiring jazz guitarist that grew each week as I saw my students.

It was an off-hand remark by a student that started me on the path of self-publishing.

"Hey Joseph, this stuff is great! You should look at publishing it."

That bounced around my head for days.

Most music books come with a CD or DVD to help the student hear what the exercises should sound like, so I sat down and recorded every exercise in my book at two speeds. The content filled three DVDs.

I sent out my manuscript to a music publisher and waited. The inevitable rejection came, but not on the grounds of my writing (which they loved). It was because it wasn't financially viable to produce a book with three DVDs. They also said that the guitar book market was dying and they were struggling to sell their own titles.

Another of my students suggested I should self-publish my work and I quickly discovered Kindle Direct Publishing (KDP), Amazon's digital self-publishing department. It took me a few days to put together a cover (which, looking back, was terrible!) and upload the book to Amazon. Through KDP I discovered CreateSpace (CS), Amazon's paperback publishing department. Suddenly I had both a Kindle and a paperback for sale.

To handle the audio side of things I bought an Internet domain (**www.fundamental-changes.com**) and uploaded the MP3s to a very basic site I built with WordPress.

Despite my terrible cover and ugly website, my book started to sell a few copies. Even more bizarrely it even got a few decent reviews. I guess there wasn't that much competition for guitar books back in 2012! In my first few months I started to make a few hundred pounds which, on top of my teaching, would make a nice little retirement contribution.

Encouraged by this success I wrote another book, and then another. Amazon started to cross-promote them and sales started to grow. I used my experience as a guitar teacher to write simple yet detailed guides, which answered the most common questions and problems I'd encountered from my students.

The most important thing to realise (which is still true today) is that I wasn't writing for the money. I wrote out of a genuine desire to help guitarists who were struggling with the same issues that had caused me so much pain as an aspiring musician. Everything was written to the best of my ability with integrity and as much value as I could cram in.

Readers responded well to my books and the rest is history. After one year I'd written eight books. As of today, six years since my first book, I've written over forty titles and they've been translated into four languages. I've also used my branding to attract other musicians and authors who publish under the Fundamental Changes label. They get a great deal and I get to expand the reach of my catalogue. I have inadvertently created a brand that has attracted hundreds of thousands of students and readers.

Currently we are expanding to encompass books on singing, bass, drums and keyboard and I have a whole team of freelancers working for me around the world to make my publishing process as smooth and streamlined as possible. We're starting to add more non-fiction tutorial books on sports and exercise, and the company is growing rapidly.

At the heart of everything is the mantra, "Have integrity, add value". My best advice is to forget about the money and concentrate on making the best possible product you can. If you get it right, the money will follow.

Tim's Story

"Tim is an amazing writer! He produced something far greater than I imagined possible. I wouldn't hesitate to use his services again."
Graham Dacre CBE, business entrepreneur

"When I was dipping my toe into writing for the first time, I knew nothing about how to get it out there. Tim was great; he came alongside, believed in what I was doing, helped to knock it all into shape and … got it out there."
Simon Ward, COO The British Fashion Council, author & speaker

* * *

I've spent the last 20 years of my life in and around the publishing business. I was always an avid reader, but eventually I realised I could edit other people's work quite successfully when I had the opportunity to help run a magazine.

The magazine was a helpful platform to get to edit my first book. I say "edit" because that's what I called it at the time. Today I would call it a "structural rewrite"! A year later I had given up my job in IT, moved south and joined my first publishing company. I completely fell in love with the process of book publishing and never looked back.

Fast forward to the present day and I've worked for several different UK publishers. Eight years ago I decided to turn freelance and worked for numerous different publishers simultaneously, both in the UK and the US. I've also ghost written around 30 books. All in all, I guess I've helped to publish around 700 titles across a wide spectrum of genres (fiction, non-fiction, religious, business, biography, autobiography and more).

A couple of anecdotes come to mind that are germane to the subject of this book.

I was standing in a large conference hall in Orlando, Florida, chatting to the publishing director of a $200 million plus international publisher. He mentioned the name of a well-known, bestselling author who he was pleased to have just acquired for his company.

"That's great," I complimented him, "what's he writing about?"

"Oh, it doesn't matter what he writes about," he replied. "He can write a cook book for all I care."

Reality check #1: "This is not the type of publishing I want to be involved in!" I thought to myself. I actually care about the content and quality of books I produce!

Authors often get very excited if a publisher becomes interested in what they are doing, but people need to go into publishing with their eyes open. There is definitely a "sausage factory" mentality that exists within professional publishing. There are some terrific publishers out there run by people who care about their authors, but equally there are some very well-known ones who mostly care about the sale. In short, working with a publisher is not all it's cracked up to be.

On another occasion, I was chatting to an author who had submitted a novel for me to review. This guy was seriously gifted. I coasted through the text in wonder at how little editing it needed. My job on this occasion was to pitch the book to a publisher for him, which I said I would have no problem in doing, given the quality of his work. Then he asked me a question which taught me a lot about writers.

"So, can you give me a rough timeline of when I'll need to give up my day job?"

In his mind, before his book had even been shown to a publisher, let alone published, he had made a huge mental leap:

- First book comes out
- First book is a bestseller
- I reap the immediate rewards of the first book's sales, buy a modest villa in Tuscany and begin drafting book two
- Book two comes out, and repeat…

Reality check #2: Many, many writers have a rose-tinted, vague, or just wildly inaccurate view of what a publisher will do for them.

There are a great many myths about publishing. Writers spend a long time toiling over their work. It's not only a big time investment, but a big emotional investment. So I like authors to be well-informed about their publishing choices. Many people *think* they need a publisher, when in reality, most don't. Here are some of the myths:

Myth 1

I need a publisher's expertise to create my book.

Not true – the skills needed to plan, write, design and publish can all be learned. The point of this book is to coach and guide you through those essential skills.

Myth 2

A publisher will promote me as an author and market my book.

I have lost count of the number of times I've heard this. The first problem with this statement is that the act of publishing a book will not result in your phone ringing all day long with invitations for after-dinner speaking engagements. You can laugh, but you'd be amazed how many people think this.

Second, publishers will spend most of their time slotting your book into their automated marketing processes (catalogues, trade press releases, sales rep briefing sheets). I can guarantee you that they are not thinking about getting you on the sofa for a cosy chat on morning TV, financing a book tour for you, or planning full-page advertising spreads in newspapers and magazines. There are good reasons why – we'll touch on them later.

Myth 3

Self-published books usually have sub-standard design, print, and content.

This used to be the case, but not anymore. Writers have sometimes looked down on self-publishing in favour of a "real" publisher because they think having the latter will give them kudos. I understand that point of view, but recent history has proven that people can create very successful publishing enterprises on their own. These people are not sitting around waiting for their phone calls to be returned or wondering what their publishers are doing with their book.

Myth 4

I need a publisher because without one, I'll have limited distribution.

This is another common fallacy. It used to be the case, but now we have a global online marketplace in which anyone can get setup and begin selling – and there are multiple points of access to the market. We'll discuss approaches to distribution later in this book.

Myth 5

I'm not capable of doing everything myself.

Some people just want to write and I get that. They prefer to have other people do the nuts and bolts work. First, you can definitely do more than you think. With a bit of guidance you'll see that it's not rocket science, you just need a well-conceived strategy.

Myth 6

Even if I work with a publisher, I'll still get the final say on how my book is edited, the cover design and other issues.

Sorry for the wake-up call, but no you won't! Publishers build into their contracts the right to veto the author's wishes on the look and feel of their book because they are the "experts". This includes how the book is edited, how it's designed, as well as how it's pitched to the market in terms of its blurb and sales description.

Many authors feel vulnerable about entrusting their work to others – many of whom are faceless entitles (apart from their editor) – and rightly so. The simple fact is, if you work with a publisher, you give up creative control.

So, can you retain creative control, but still get a top quality professional result? Yes, you can!

Myth 7

If I work with a publisher I'll sell more books and make a fortune.

There is so much wrong with this statement I barely know where to begin, but let me say this:

First, as a self-published author you'll keep the majority of the revenue from your book sales. With a traditional publisher you'll earn between 10–15% of net revenue after costs, maximum. You'll have to sell A LOT of books to get rich.

Second, it's not a given that your book will sell, and there will be very little that you personally can do about it. If you feel that the publisher didn't quite "get" the content and therefore didn't pitch it right, tough! This is the risk of traditional publishing.

Third, it's possible to set up global distribution for your book on your own, without the help of a publisher. There are many bestselling, self-published authors who have sold millions of copies of their work, without the assistance of a traditional publisher.

I hope this brief overview helps to set the scene for what's to come. Publishing can be a bit of a minefield, but there is a wealth of information and publishing advice on our website if you want to go deeper. Meanwhile, let's get on with helping you to write your book!

Part One:
Planning, Writing, Editing, Formatting & Publishing Your Book

Chapter One: How *Not* to Write your First Book

As you're reading this book you probably already have an idea about your writing topic. You may be thinking, "I want to write a book about X."

"X" is probably your main area of interest, expertise or passion.

Most writers who come to us for advice usually have a fairly fixed idea in mind about what they want to write. In our experience, this can be a mistake that puts limits on someone's potential as a successful self-published author.

"Surely it's good to have a clear idea of what I want to write about?" we hear you protest.

Yes and no.

There are a number of factors to consider before you put pen to paper.

Over the last few years we've seen hundreds of book proposals come across our desks. After a while you see the trends. People tend to make the same mistakes over and again. The truth is, most books don't flop because the author is a terrible writer (though sometimes they are!), but because the book concept is flawed. Here is how NOT to write your book:

1. Write in a vacuum

There are lots of talented writers out there producing some great books, but if you want to sell books and become successful, you need to start thinking more like a publisher. By writing in a vacuum we mean writing without giving any thought to the market or the audience you're aiming at – you are just focused on what you are creating. But you've got to do some homework before you begin.

There are two ways in which you might write in a vacuum:

a) **A lack of market awareness.** You conceive an incredible, genre-busting idea with a great twist, then spend hundreds of hours writing the book, only to discover that someone thought of it first. Be aware of who has written about what in your genre and what has been successful. If you're passionate about a particular topic, one of the keys to success for you will be showing readers why your book is different.

b) Writing for over-published areas. If you want to write in an already heavily published area, make sure you have something fresh to say, or be confident that you can put a brand new spin on a familiar subject. In the area of business literature, Seth Godin broke the mould of the generic management / marketing handbook with his book *Purple Cow: Transform Your Business by Being Remarkable.* It has since been copied a great deal, but at the time there was literally nothing like it, so it stood out.

It's hard to come up with unique ideas, of course, and there's nothing wrong with writing for a niche that has already been widely written for, if that's your passion. For example, you might want to write a business book, or a vampire-based thriller. Both have been well served already. This just means that if you want your book to stand out, you'll need to up your game when it comes to the writing, or find a slightly different spin to other books.

2. Write a soft focus book

The easiest books to market are those with a very clear purpose or message that can be easily described (bearing in mind the caveat of point 1). We often ask authors to sum up the central message of their book in no more than 100 words. This is a good exercise to do because it forces people to crystallise the most important message they have and do away with anything peripheral. If you are struggling to describe the main theme of your book in 100 words, it's very likely you are trying to address too many issues.

A soft focus book takes a broad topic and examines lots of different aspects superficially. A sharp focus book takes a single theme, or one aspect of a larger topic, and examines it thoroughly. Even if you are writing a novel, think about your overriding theme. A good starting point is often to write your back cover blurb first, so that you remember to keep the main thing, *the main thing.*

3. Don't think about your audience. It's essential to understand who you are trying to reach with your writing. Readers tend to group together around topics, or fiction genres they love, so who is it that you are going after? Often authors are clear about the "what", but not so much the "who". For instance, you may say, "I'd like my book to be read and enjoyed by people of all ages." But the fact is, *very* few books fall into that category. You're not J.K. Rowling or A.A. Milne. Booksellers have multiple categories for describing books and they target very specific niches (science fantasy for 9-12 year olds, for instance), so you need to be really clear about it.

Research the niche you are writing for. Who are the bestselling authors? How do they pitch their books (and themselves) to the market? Learn from those who are doing it successfully. Decide on your target audience *before* you begin writing and keep that audience in mind as you develop your book.

4. Write for current trends. We've met lots of authors who've thought, "Wow, this thing is really in vogue at the moment, I'll write about that." It's tempting to write about stuff that is currently trending, but there are two problems with this approach. First, unless you are the sort of person who can spot a trend and write about it before it becomes common knowledge, then the chances are someone else will beat you to it. One of the reasons why a topic is currently in vogue is that media outlets have been talking about it. Unless you have something really original to say about it, it's likely to be old news by the time you get your book out. Second, this type of book is usually a fad book and it will have a finite shelf life. Ideally, you should be planning to write books that will still be selling years from now.

5. Write your magnum opus. Often authors will sit down to write and attempt to throw everything they have at a book to make it their *magnum opus* (Latin for "great work" or masterpiece). However, you need to plan your book carefully and only include things that are truly relevant to the subject matter. Work hard to keep on topic with your writing and don't be tempted to go on "interesting" diversions. They may be interesting for you, but can make it hard for the reader to follow your narrative thread. Authors sometimes feel that they are adding value by packing tons of information into their book, but we'll explain why this is a flawed approach with a little story from Joseph.

* * *

I was approached by a friend who said he wanted to write a book on "bass guitar". Let's call him John. John is an astonishingly good bass player – an in-demand London-based musician, writer, teacher and performer. I jammed with him regularly at music college, so I know he's the real deal. After we had reconnected and I'd checked out his teaching website and YouTube videos, we had a conversation about the book he wanted to write for my Fundamental Changes publishing imprint.

"So, basically, I want to write a book on bass guitar," he said.

"What, all of it?" I responded.

"Err, yes?!" he said.

After a few probing questions, however, I ascertained that John didn't want to write about funk, rock, blues or orchestral bass. It wasn't going to be a book on technique (although that would be part of it) and he didn't want to cover theory too much either.

After several minutes I helped him to conclude that the main focus of his book would be teaching people how to really *groove* on the bass. I thought this was a great idea, so we took the next step and I asked John to write a chapter outline for the book and plan how he would approach it (we'll discuss planning and chapter outlines in the next chapter).

In due course John's book was published and now it is selling nicely.

* * *

The real benefit of this conversation was that the author suddenly saw the potential to write multiple books about his passion, focusing on one distinct aspect each time and going in-depth.

You may want to write a book about a given subject, but is that subject so small and specific that all the essentials can be covered in *just one book*?

Joseph has written 40+ books about guitar playing. Each one targets a specific aspect of music and goes deep into that topic. The result is a series of books that is highly specific and meets very clear needs. Potential customers can look at those books and say, "Hey, that's exactly what I'm looking for!"

Consider your topic. By dividing up what you want to say into shorter, more detailed volumes you will write better books. You will also increase your chances of publishing success by developing a growing relationship with your readers. Simply put, you'll just sell more books!

Don't play the game of some publishers who pump out overpriced books with not much content. If you're writing a non-fiction book, it should be nothing less than brilliant; informative, great to read, and packed with genuinely useful information. If you're writing fiction, it should be well-crafted, well-conceived, engaging and unputdownable. But pace yourself. If you set out to write *War and Peace*, the chances are you'll just never finish it.

We hope we've explained why attempting to write one definitive book is not the way to go about becoming a self-publishing success. Take the long view. If you're writing a novel, consider how it might be developed into a series. If you're writing non-fiction, break the idea down into its constituent parts and think how it could become an in-depth series that links together.

Having just one book can make the task of marketing an uphill struggle. One book is like a needle in a haystack in an online store like Amazon. Even if your book is excellent, there is no particular reason why someone should buy it, even if they manage to stumble across it. By writing multiple books that focus on different topics of your chosen subject / genre, you are giving yourself a much greater chance of being discovered.

In the next chapter we'll look together at how to come up with a book idea and how to plan and structure your work.

Chapter Two: Conceiving, Planning and Structuring your Book

A blank sheet of paper can be a terrifying thing, but most people would love to be able to write a book and have a few ideas kicking around. Writing a book need not be a daunting task if it's tackled the right way, but so much of it is in the planning.

We would go as far as to say that 70% of writing a great book is in writing a rock solid chapter outline. Once a well-conceived framework is in place, the actual writing is so much easier. If you'd like to write a book, but are not sure how to approach it, this chapter is for you.

Generating book ideas

Writers draw inspiration from all kinds of places. In the fiction genre, an overheard snippet of conversation in a café might provide the impetus for a plot idea. In the travel genre, a visit to a particular place that included some surprising discoveries might give you the ammunition to write a guide to the lesser known attractions of that place.

In the non-fiction music genre Fundamental Changes is known for, we've sometimes used a simple spreadsheet to generate ideas. The columns are headed:

Style or genre | Instrument | Topic | Ability level

Just by filling in the columns, you can probably see how this can quickly generate some simple but useful ideas. E.g. a book on pop piano playing for beginners. How about a rock guitar scales book for the advanced guitarist? Or a book that teaches alternate tuning folk guitar to beginners?

Style/Genre	Topic	Ability Level	Instrument
Rock	Soloing	Beginner	Electric Guitar
Jazz	Scales	Intermediate	Acoustic Guitar
Blues	Theory	Advanced	Bass
Classical	Technique	Kid	Piano
Funk	Chords	Left Handed	Keyboard
Pop	Sightreading		Voice
RnB	Groove		Drums
Folk	Alternate Tunings		
Heavy Metal			

For fiction, your spreadsheet could have different headings but serve a similar purpose:

Protagonist | Time period or setting | Problem or challenge | Target audience

Ideas that could be generated by this grid might be...

1. An Internet security expert working for present day MI6 finds that a large amount of sensitive data has been compromised and the race is on to retrieve it before it falls into the wrong hands. Aimed at readers who enjoy Tom Clancy books.

Or,

2. Set around the medieval castles of Kent, an historical novel traces the fortunes of a warrior / priest who is facing up to his own dark past while searching for his lost sister. Aimed at readers of Ken Follett's *Pillars of the Earth*.

Protagonist	Period / Setting	Problem	Target Audience
MI6 security analyst	Modern day London	Loss of sensitive data threatens a national security crisis	Tom Clancy thriller readers
Warrior/Priest	Medieval Britain	Conflicted lead character searches for his missing sister	Historical adventure fiction

Hopefully you can see that this is a very quick and creative way of generating ideas. Have a brainstorming session for your area of writing and see what you come up with. If no single idea sticks, then mix and match the best ideas you came up with to create some new ones. By combining ideas like this, it's possible to come up with hundreds of potential book plots. Use the spreadsheet as a "book generator" and keep recording your ideas until inspiration strikes.

Let's take a different topic, say cooking. Initial thoughts for book ideas might revolve around countries, specific cooking techniques, specific food groups (noodles, pasta, chicken, fish), or the nutritional needs of certain types of people.

Country/Region	Technique	Meal	Main Ingredient	Audience
Italian	Fry/Wok	Breakfast	Beef	Beginner
Chinese	Baking	Lunch	Chicken	Intermediate
French	Streaming	Dinner	Vegetables	Advanced
Indian	Microwave	Snacks	Eggs	Student
British	Oven	Desserts	Lamb	Single Parent
Spanish	Boiling	Party Food	Pork	Busy Family
Mexican		Large Groups	Pasta	Religious Requirements
Eastern European			Rice	Allergies
Thai				

By now, you get the idea and can come up with your own spreadsheet headings, but a brainstorming session might produce:

- Easy Italian Meals for Busy People
- The Vegan Runner's Protein Book
- Great Tasting Low-Carb Meals on a Budget, or
- Kosher Cookery for Students

Again, mixing and matching the elements above will yield a bigger list of potential ideas.

Your job *right now* is to carry out this exercise with your chosen subject. Spend some time on it and have fun. Think about your column headings, but then throw down anything relevant onto each list.

For the fiction writer, once you've settled on the basic plot, you could create a second, enhanced spreadsheet with more columns, that drills down in the detail a bit more. The headings might be:

Protagonist | Protagonist's character or interests | Time period or setting | Problem or challenge | Antagonist | Antagonist's aim or desire

To use the earlier example, this enhanced book idea might read:

An Internet security expert is working for present day MI6. She suffers from agoraphobia and is most happy in the confines of her underground office. She discovers a large amount of sensitive data has been compromised and the race is on to retrieve it before it falls into the wrong hands. Eager to get his hands on the data is a former Mossad agent, now working for an Israeli weapons dealer. Our heroine will find herself tested to the limits of her ingenuity and forced out of her comfort zone.

Alternately the heading could include specific locations you know you can write about, emotional issues, journeys from one place to another, relationships and more. You get the idea.

This simple process achieves several important aims:

1) You will be able to come up with more creative ideas for your given subject and your writing is likely to be more diverse and engaging.

2) Writing your books will become easier, because your starting point is a simple, focused idea. You'll pay more attention to making each book work on its own merits and your readers will have a better experience and be more likely to buy another of your books.

3) When it comes to marketing your books, having a series of books will make your writing more discoverable. If you have multiple titles, sellers like Amazon will cross promote your books and this will ultimately help you sell more copies.

On this latter point, at the time of writing, Fundamental Changes has sold over 400,000 books via Amazon. What is interesting is that those sales have not been linear. The more books we've published, the more sales have grown for the older titles as well as the new ones. Because of the cross-promotion Amazon does, combined with our automated email marketing (this will be covered in detail in a later chapter), the sales have gained momentum over time.

Each book you publish is like a business card. If people like it, they'll come back for more. In marketing, the first sale is always the hardest. Changing someone from a casual browser into a customer is a big step. Once that customer comes to view you as a brand they can trust, it is much easier to sell them another product. Especially if that product is useful to them and accurately targeted to their specific interests.

Amazon is incredibly good at showing people things they want to buy. You can mimic this by building a clever mailing list, so that your readers will only be shown the books they're interested in. For example, we're not going to send a Heavy Metal advert to someone we know is interested in Jazz guitar. But we're getting ahead of ourselves...!

In the past we've taken clients we've mentored through this process when they've been stuck for ideas. The book generation spreadsheet is so effective that in some instances, the number of ideas generated was almost overwhelming. But don't worry, you don't have to write every book! You will, however, write a much more focused book using this method. The fiction book plot above was described using just *90 words*. Yes, 90, and yet it's a pretty clear outline for a book and you can use your imagination to fill in the rest of the plot.

Which book should I write first?

Once you have been through the idea generation process, the next step is to focus on the list. Keep a copy of the full list of ideas for future reference, but make a separate copy and pick out those you feel are the best ideas. Whittle your list down to the top five ideas, then consider each one on its own merits.

Out of those five, which book should you write first? Our advice is to start with the easiest. Start with the one you are most passionate about. There will be one idea in your list of possible books that focuses on something you care about and are excited to cover.

It may be that you're passionate about environmental issues, so you make your novel's protagonist an environmental lobbyist based in

Washington. You can start with this idea and write about what you know.

It could be that you're a sax player who has a large collection of music from the Blue Note Records jazz era, so you decide to write a book of saxophone lines and riffs in the style of your heroes, such as Cannonball Adderley, Sonny Rollins, John Coltrane and Dexter Gordon.

One title will jump out at you and this will be the easiest book to write because a) you're passionate about the subject matter, b) you're knowledgeable about the topic, and c) you'll have the most energy and enthusiasm to complete it.

An American publishing colleague of ours used to commission books for a large publisher and used some very simple criteria to judge whether a manuscript was worth pursuing. Our explanations are in brackets.

1. Does it have integrity? (Is it well conceived, logical, flowing and well written?)

2. Is it authentic? (Does the author *really* know what they are talking about?)

3. Can we sell it? (Is there a market for it?)

One of your book ideas should have come to the top, and you'll already be thinking about what you'll say, how you'll tackle the subject, and what you might include. If it's a non-fiction title, that might include helpful diagrams, images and bonus content. You'll be considering how you can add value to readers and maintain momentum, so they are motivated to keep turning the pages. It doesn't take a rocket scientist to identify that *this* is the book with which you should begin your writing career.

The planning process

Abraham Lincoln once said, "Give me six hours to chop down a tree and I will spend the first four sharpening the axe." It's all about the planning!

1. Mind mapping

For now, give your book a working title that describes its content and, if you can think of one, a complementary subtitle. The final title and subtitle can come later (though it's surprising how many of our "working" titles have made it to final publication) – the last thing you want to get hung up on before you begin writing is trying to come up with a catchy title. The most important task now is to plan your book's content.

If you know your subject matter well (for non-fiction), or you have summarised your plot as above (for fiction), then the next step is to get your ideas on paper. Grab a pen and a blank sheet of paper. Yes, we did just say that. Don't complete this task using a spreadsheet or a piece of "efficiency" software. Your initial ideas should be free flowing and "unstructured". You are just capturing ideas. Computers and tablets / iPads are barriers in this process. Just scribble ideas straight from your brain to paper.

Create a mind map that begins with you writing your working title in the centre of the page. Now brainstorm every important aspect of your topic.

Non-fiction writers: list every facet of the subject you intend to cover and connect them via lines to the centre. E.g. Thai Cooking = the essential spices; cooking methods; typical ingredients; recipe lists etc.

Fiction writers: list the details of the main characters, where the action will take place, important plot points, key events etc.

Try to include every bit of information that seems vital to the book. If a word or phrase is critical to you, circle or highlight that word so that it stands out. Make sure you capture all the important ideas and jot down a few bullet points under each, to remind yourself of what you'll cover in that part of the book. Aim for about 10 main ideas and have 3 or 4 points that summarise each idea.

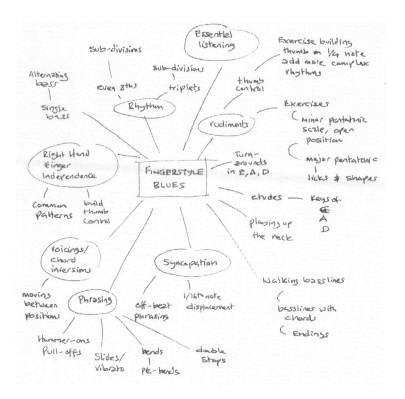

Above is the mind map Joseph created for his book, *Fingerstyle Blues Guitar*. The map may not make sense to you (even if you're a guitarist!), but that's the point really. It provided Joseph with all the stimulus and reminders *he* needed to be able to write the book from start to finish in under three weeks (and that included recording studio quality audio for every example). This mind map was translated into a comprehensive outline which formed the basis of the book.

Fingerstyle Blues Guitar came out just in time for the Christmas 2015 rush and has since been translated into three other languages and has netted around $60,000. Not bad for three weeks' work.

Fingerstyle Blues Guitar continues to sell well and is one of our favourite books because it is well structured, goes into great depth, and takes the student from first principles on a journey to becoming a competent Delta Blues guitarist. It's certainly not the best selling Fundamental Changes title, but it is an extremely effective one.

2. From mind-map to plan

Now you've got your mind map, which is likely only decipherable by you, how can it be turned into a cohesive book plan? It just take a bit of organisation.

You have mapped out all your ideas, now spend some time considering, a) which are the most important and b) the logical order in which they should appear.

If you were writing a non-fiction book that offered a creative solution to a common problem, then a logical progression for your book might be:

- Explain the problem, looking at it from various angles
- Hint at the solution you've found (without fully expanding on it at this stage)
- Begin to unveil your solution in subsequent chapters, revealing layer upon layer
- In the penultimate chapter, show the reader the entire solution
- In the final chapter, show the reader how they can successfully apply it for themselves

The most important ideas in your mind map will become your chapter titles, because they represent the main areas of focus for your book. If you're writing non-fiction, aim for about 10 chapters. Now list 3 or 4 strongly related points under each heading. Make sure each point really does relate, and you're not throwing in any red herrings just because you've nowhere else to put them.

If you happen to be writing a cook book containing only beef recipes, the chances are your first chapter will be called "All About Beef" and will discuss all the different cuts of beef that are available; how beef is aged for flavour; how to source the best beef; sustainable farming, and so on.

Coming back to the *Fingerstyle Blues Guitar* book, it was essential that the first chapter covered the technical aspects of this style. Without going into too much detail, this style of playing relies very heavily on the picking hand. Trying to teach this style without first addressing this issue would be confusing and frustrating for the reader!

The mind map entry called "R/H Finger Independence" became a chapter called "Rudiments and Finger Independence" and covered all the abilities a student would need to develop if they wanted to master this style: Basic Thumb Control, Finger Independence, Playing Different Rhythms, and Introducing Simple Melodies.

Below is the final list of chapter headings for *Fingerstyle Blues Guitar* that resulted from the mind map.

Part One: Finger Independence and Soloing

Chapter One: Rudiments and Finger Independence

Chapter Two: Introducing Scales and Soloing

   - Bends

   - Second position soloing

   - Slides and double stops

Chapter Three: Legato and Vibrato

   - Vibrato

Chapter Four: Syncopation

Chapter Five: Triplet Feel

Chapter Six: The Major Pentatonic Scale

   - Moveable shapes

Part Two: Rhythm Guitar Vocabulary, Patterns and Techniques

Chapter Seven: Chords, Strumming and Basic Patterns

   - Fingerpicking patterns

Chapter Eight: Combining Melodies, Chords and Bass lines

Chapter Nine: Playing up the Neck

   - Voicings and Inversions

Chapter Ten: Turnarounds, Endings, and Bass Lines

   - Bass lines With Chords

Studies

Essential Listening

After mulling over the mind map, the book fell neatly into two halves and a natural, logical order for the chapters emerged. The beauty of this method is that it gives you a clear guide from which to write the book, simply by expanding on the chapters and subtopics in front of you. You need never struggle with writer's block, because if one part is proving difficult now, you can easily take a break, jump into another topic and return to it later.

One final tip before we move on. A chapter outline is a great guide and will give you direction and keep you on track. That said, don't be afraid to revise it if you suddenly realise you've missed out ideas you want to include. You will probably also find that the act of writing generates other good ideas that aren't necessarily for this book. Write them down and keep them somewhere safe. Chances are they'll go in your next book.

How long should your book be?

This is a bit of a "How long is a piece of string?" question, but it is a very common question people ask, so we will endeavour to give you some rough guidelines. The first thing to say, however, is that the final page count of a book is of much greater relevance than its word count, for reasons that will become apparent in a moment. We'll deal with the areas of non-fiction and fiction separately.

1. Non-fiction tuition books

The music tuition books published by Fundamental Changes are published in large format: 8.5" x 11" (21.59 x 27.94cm) – the biggest size KDP can accommodate and one which Amazon can fulfil via their Prime program (so that customers receive the book within 24hrs of ordering). Due to combining many musical examples with the narrative, they don't have large word counts. Joseph recalls paying a lot of money for a jazz study book years ago and being disappointed to find it was only 36 pages long. It was still a great book, but not great value for money. It left him feeling that he wanted to make his own books really good value for money, so for the same price the customer would receive a book around three times as long.

The critical factor is not how many words the books contain, but how many pages they are. All of Fundamental Changes music books range from 90 to 106 pages in length. Why 106 pages? All our books are published via Amazon's print-on-demand (POD) service, Kindle Direct Publishing (KDP). Beyond the 106-page threshold, Amazon charges a small fee for every additional page printed, which of course increases the production cost, but more importantly dilutes the royalty income. Call us cheap, but after selling over 400,000 books, those extra cents really start to add up!

We have arrived at our current publishing model after some trial and error and much consideration about what works best. It works well for us, though personally we think that circa 106 pages is a good size for any kind of tuition book. Your specific area of publishing might necessitate a slightly different approach.

2. Other types of non-fiction

Tuition books are a very specific publishing niche, so what about other types of non-fiction book? This might include genres such as travel guides, self-help, spirituality, biographies, business (and all its sub-genres, such as management, marketing, sales techniques, entrepreneurship etc), true crime and many more. There are no hard and fast rules, but there are some ballpark guidelines.

- Self-help and spirituality books tend to be lighter reads, typically around 150 pages, which equates to 35,000 – 40,000 words. Such books retail for around £7.99 / $11.99

- Business books tend to be a bit weightier, perhaps on the presumption that shrewd business people want more value for money. These books tend to be in the 40,000 – 60,000 word range and circa 200 pages. Retail prices will be around £12.00 / $18.00

- Biographies or autobiographies will be longer still, typically somewhere between 70,000 and 90,000 words and can be up to 500 pages long. Interestingly, this is one of the publishing niches where the retail price is not directly proportionate to the number of pages. A brand new biography of the comedian Robin Williams, published in 2018, is 560 pages long, published in hardback, yet retails for just £14. This area of publishing is considered to have a specific shelf life – celebrities are in the news, then they're not. The publishers go nuts while they are, but accept that the transient nature of fame makes their publishing less predictable.

3. Fiction

Historically, novels have tended to have fairly large word counts, usually anywhere between 100,000 and 150,000 words. Each of Tolkien's *Lord of the Rings* books weighs in at around 100k, though *The Fellowship of the Ring* has over 177k words. Again, fiction is one of those niches where the retail price doesn't reflect the epic effort that goes into writing the books. You can pick up the aforementioned Tolkien book for £6 / $9.

Don't get too hung up on the numbers though. They are a guide to what's happening in the marketplace, but often only because of arbitrary decisions made by book publishers. You need not be limited by them. Many successful novelists are producing shorter works that are selling hundreds of thousands of copies (circa 50-60,000 words) and generally there is a market trend towards shorter books.

It can be extremely daunting to think, "I'm writing a novel, so I've got to produce over 100,000 words!" If that seems like a mountain to climb, you could write a shorter novella instead, or a collection of short stories. If you're self-publishing, then you are the boss, so by all means go with your gut instinct.

As with most things in life, it's good to have a clear goal. Tim has edited hundreds of authors over the years and offers this advice about hitting your target length:

If you're writing a self-help type book, which you want to be around 35,000 words, but you've got a lot to say, don't be afraid to write more. It's always easier to sharpen up a text by deleting words and distilling the message down to its essentials, than it is to pad out a text that has too few words for its readership. The former method is likely to produce a good book, full of good content that doesn't waste words. The latter is likely to be filled with irrelevant fluff.

All of these guidelines are useful, but when you are planning and writing your book, the thing you should be most concerned with is writing great content that will be valuable to the reader. The most common sizes for trade paperbacks are 5.5" x 8.5" and 6" x 9", but that is not something that should concern you while you're writing your novel! Words can easily be formatted for print later.

Most of our circa 100-page books tend to contain between 15,000 and 20,000 words. Some, however (the ones with tons of notated musical examples) can be as low as 8,000 words. One example of this is a book that has a lot of scale diagrams and guitar licks. It sells fantastically well and no one has ever complained that it didn't have enough words in it! All they care about is whether it delivers what it promises, teaches them what they want to know, and adds value to their musical life.

When it comes to words, often less is more. A line often attributed to Hemmingway reads as follows:

"For sale: baby shoes, never worn."

There is a powerful, troubling story, told in just 6 words. A book with a bigger word count doesn't mean a book that is more effective, and often the opposite will be true.

Word count does *not* equate to value.

Fortunately, the self-published author doesn't need to jump through industry hoops dreamt up by publishers, so we don't need to care too much about it. What we do care about is happy customers who go on to champion our work, because this is the lifeblood of successful publishing. We'll talk more about audience building and your relationship with your readers in a later chapter. The bottom line is that you should give your readers as much value as possible. Pack your book with useful information, or a gripping storyline, have integrity in your craft and you won't go far wrong.

Chapter Three: How to Write your First Book

We all write best at different times of the day and in different creative settings. The bottom line is that you need to find a writing rhythm that works for you and is both productive and satisfying. Here's what works for us.

Joseph

I like to get up at around 6:30am on a writing day and get a couple of hours writing in while the house is quiet. I focus well during the morning and my attention wanes throughout the day. As I write, I'm not worrying too much about hitting a specific word count, more about cramming in as much value as I can.

Because my books contain lots of musical notation I spend time thinking of examples, guitar licks and exercises that teach the subject. I notate these in professional music notation programs like Sibelius, Guitar Pro and Neck Diagrams, as well as editing some images using Photoshop.

Thinking of examples and notating them is a time-consuming task, so often I'll first plan the chapter, write and notate the examples, then write the prose once I'm happy with the overall arc of the teaching. When I write the text I leave space for each musical example and import the notation one chapter at a time.

This production line approach saves me a great deal of time because I do not have to constantly flick between programs on the computer, changing tasks between writing, creating music, notating, importing and editing. This system allows me to concentrate on just one part of the creative process at a time without having to change focus.

In the morning I find I can come into the office and sit for probably two hours (with a short break every 15 minutes to stand up and stretch) before I start to lose focus. At that point, it's time for breakfast and a shower.

I was recently invited to present at the Amazon Academy in London to around 100 writers. I spoke about my writing schedule as described above, and one of the other writers on the panel leant over to me and said,

"You don't have children, do you?!"

Well the answer is obviously, no, I don't! This is why it's important for you to find your own rhythm for writing that works around the complexities of your daily life. What works for me won't necessarily work for you.

Tim

For me, it's irrelevant what time of day I write, as long as I can achieve around 3-4 hours of uninterrupted quiet. Late at night is as good as early in the morning. That said, I must be a strangely wired person, because I can write just as well on a laptop in a noisy coffee shop. Somehow, the hubbub of conversation gets screened out and I can focus just on the words I'm writing. I find that a change of scenery from time to time helps, rather than hinders my writing process, and can produce fresh inspiration when needed.

For me, momentum is important in writing. I like to get on a roll and feel that the words are flowing; I'm capturing ideas and getting them down. To that end, I write in a two-part process. The first part is all about establishing flow and getting the ideas down. I don't agonise over sentences or worry too much about things as long as I'm writing to a good chapter outline. In the second part, I become my own editor and, wearing a different hat, go back and refine my work, tidying up the grammar and making sure that everything reads smoothly.

Different authors have different ways of dealing with the task of writing. Stephen King advocates having a private room that no else is allowed in – a place you can go to dream and jot down ideas. King prefers to start writing at about the same time each day and only leaves when he's hit a certain number of words. Maya Angelou would write all morning then take a shower at midday, do some cooking, go and perform other mundane chores, then read what she'd written in the evening, after dinner. She said, "If I'd written nine pages that morning, I might be able to save two and a half or three of them." She judged her work in a highly critical manner in order to weed out any rubbish and be left with – in her words – what was "acceptable"!

Some people need a couple of hours to "warm up" to their writing and achieve the momentum they need, while others seem able to write in short bursts. Speaking for myself and Joseph, I know that what bugs us most is being interrupted while writing, and if that's true for us, it must be true for others. Find your writing space, then guard it!

Dealing with distractions

You want to write, but what do you do if you have a day job, work shifts, have other people who require your attention, or any number of obstacles to creativity?

At the risk of seeming insensitive, the only solution we've seen other writers use that actually works is to insist on the importance of being given uninterrupted time to write. In an ideal world, the people around you would see that writing is an important creative expression of who you are as a person. But we don't live in an ideal world and you may have to negotiate for the couple of hours you need.

Some writers have a rule that when their door is shut, there can be no interruptions. We can't know whether such a rule is realistic in your situation, so we advise you to beg, steal or borrow the time you need, any way you can. Do whatever it takes. Bargain by taking on extra chores. Force yourself to get up an hour earlier than normal. If the writing means enough to you, you'll find the time one way or another.

One of the most helpful things you can do to prevent being distracted is to turn off the social media. We live in one of the most "interruptible" times in history, where instant global communication is at its peak, and people can get hold of others 24/7. Get off the Internet. Stay away from Facebook, Twitter, Instagram, Snapchat and anything else they've invented while we weren't looking. They may be fun, but they are also pointless time-suckers when it comes down to it.

Facebook is particularly addictive because we get a little endorphin hit every time that little notification pops up with someone liking our post. Block Facebook, at least while you're working. Sorry, Facebook! If you find it difficult to discipline yourself not to keep checking your social media, there are site blocking extensions you can add to your web browser to limit access to social media sites for a few hours a day. Even if you can't live without Facebook, you can learn to live without it while you're writing. Turn your phone off and leave it in another room.

Doing this may feel weird for a few days, because social media is such a huge part of our lives, but once it's been reduced, even for a few hours a day, you'll really notice a difference in your productivity, wellbeing and clarity of thought.

A few years ago Joseph was living near the beach and writing in Thailand. There was a huge storm and the Internet went down for a week. This heralded probably the most productive time in his writing career. With zero online distraction, a great deal of writing got done in a much shorter space of time than usual! If you can manage it, literally turn off the Internet while you write and you'll quickly feel the benefit.

The Writing Process

You know by now that, although we have dabbled in fiction, the bulk of our publishing is in the area of non-fiction. The following advice therefore applies mostly to non-fiction authors, though the principles of good writing hold true for any genre. If you would like the input of a master fiction editor, we recommend getting hold of the book *Stein on Writing* by Sol Stein (ISBN 9780312254216).

Joseph on non-fiction
Ten years ago, I was working as a SCUBA diving instructor in Thailand. One phrase that was used a lot (apart from, "Gin and tonic, please"), was "Plan your dive, then dive your plan."

The previous chapter showed how to mind-map a book and organise the chaos into meaningful chapters and subtopics. With a strong plan of your book, all that remains is to write it.

Throughout, you will add different ideas that aren't in the plan, reorganise the structure and make various other small alterations, but the general content and direction should remain the same. Have this plan on a piece of paper in front of you and don't be afraid to add new sections (or lose bits!) as you go along.

For me, having a plan means that writing is simply a case of filling in the detailed information and exercises I want to use, to best help students achieve their goals. On my book plan I see a short sentence describing a topic and now my job is to elaborate on it.

My secret is this: I write as I teach, and I've been teaching for years.

I'm fortunate to be an experienced teacher. I've come across most challenges that a student can throw at me and, because of this, I can pre-empt them. This helps me problem solve in my books by anticipating and addressing common issues the reader may experience.

When writing, I imagine a student sitting in front of me with their guitar. I match their ability with the target audience of my book and write as if I was teaching that student how to accomplish their goal.

I think very carefully about my approach when writing a tuition guide, because the reader doesn't get to ask me questions or give me feedback – I have to anticipate their questions and the hurdles they may face. For this reason, I take a "zero to hero" approach in my writing. It's important for me to assume my reader has a basic level of ability and understanding on the guitar.

This level will change depending on the content of the book, but I normally choose a "virtual student" who can play a few chords, scales, and could probably play a song to a decent degree. This prevents me having to start each book with, "OK, so this is a guitar and here is how you hold it…"

I start writing chapter one with the basic exercises the student will need to master the material, then guide them by the hand, incrementally, through increasingly involved examples until they have mastered everything they need for that chapter. I then continue into chapter two by building on the work in chapter one, or introducing another basic exercise in a related area.

Sometimes I feel that the first chapter may be a little simple for some readers, but it is better that they skip a small part of my book than be completely alienated by difficult examples on page 1. Of course, this is rarely a concern if the book is explicitly aimed at advanced students.

In summary, I find the best way to write an expository book is to imagine your target audience sitting in front of you. Write as if you were speaking to them. Before you write, ask yourself, "How would I explain this idea?" Better still, go and find a willing victim to experiment on. You'll have some immediate feedback, find out where you're not clear in your ideas, and quickly learn how to convey the subject clearly without digression.

Remember, small manageable steps create happy readers who get to feel a constant sense of achievement.

Tim on non-fiction

A lot of the advice that Joseph has shared about writing instructional guides holds true for other types of non-fiction. If you are essentially teaching people something (how to meditate, how to succeed at business, how to grow Bonsai trees), certain elements should be present, regardless of the subject matter:

- Empathy with the reader
- Anticipating the objections / problems / challenges they may face in doing what you're telling them to do
- Delivering the message in a logical order, with clarity
- Keeping the content interesting

For certain types of non-fiction I would add a further thought: ensure you keep the main theme alive. For example, if you were writing a book about hill walking, you might logically include information on: the health benefits of walking; equipment you'll need if you want to take walking seriously; the best walks in different areas of the country;

where to find walking clubs; how to build up to tackling some of the most iconic walking routes, etc.

These are quite diverse topics that all relate to the topic of walking. How can that be turned into a cohesive piece of work without it becoming a rambling mess? (Forgive me, couldn't resist the pun!)

With a book that is wide ranging in its scope, I advocate the "coat hanger" approach. If you bought a wardrobe and discovered it had no rail inside, you'd open the door to be greeted by a jumble of coat hangers that had to be sifted through – utter chaos! Having a rail means you can hang stuff on it, decide what order it goes in, and impose some kind of system.

In the same way, the theme of your book should be like the rail on which you hang your diverse topics. It provides a constant, clearly visible backbone to your work. When you write, keep the theme on the surface and explain how the information you impart in each chapter relates to the overall theme and goal of the book.

But how do you *actually write* your book?

There are hundreds of books available on writing technique. So many, in fact, that it can be hard to find one which really resonates with you, and which actually helps to improve *your* writing technique. Most of these books, however, are giving similar advice. We've taken a bit of space here to distil the Top 10 most frequently repeated principles and put our own spin on them.

1. Have a point. That might sound harsh, but when writing it's very easy to fall into the trap of trying to sound authoritative without saying very much. The best writing takes a simple point and makes it very clearly. Don't get bogged down in irrelevancies or write words simply to fill up space.

2. Use simple language. Tim recalls reading the autobiography of a famous musician. The first half of the book read like he had swallowed a thesaurus. Unwieldy and unlikely words were thrown into the mix and it was hard to imagine they were there for any reason other than to "impress". They didn't, it just made it read awkwardly. In the second half of the book they got over themselves and it became an enjoyable read.

One thing that is characteristic of Joseph's writing style is simple, clear language, that says what it means and means what it says. Why *facilitate someone's cognitive processes* when you can simply *help them to understand?*

3. Express one idea per sentence. One of Tim's bugbears as an editor is seeing writers try to cram several ideas into the same sentence. When authors say, "I can't make this sentence sound right," it's usually because they need to break apart the ideas and express them in different sentences.

4. Short sentences and short paragraphs. Short sentences and paragraphs tend to make for a clear, uncluttered style of writing. Fiction writers Lee Child and James Patterson both use very short sentences, lots of paragraph breaks and, indeed, quite short chapters in their writing. This technique makes for impactful prose that is dynamic and fast moving.

If you can stick to the rule of having one idea per sentence, then the bigger picture is to stick to one concept per paragraph. If you want to change topic, mark the change with a paragraph break. That way it's abundantly clear to the reader where you are going. Your overall theme will link the paragraphs together, but your content should be broken into bite-sized chunks. Especially when writing non-fiction, a large part of your job is breaking down the material into easily digestible ideas.

5. Show don't tell. This one aptly applies very much to fiction writers, but holds true for non-fiction too. Anton Chekhov said, "Don't tell me the moon is shining; show me the glint of light on broken glass." Fiction writers, make your writing come alive with engaging description and vivid characters. Don't feel you have to describe every aspect of a character; show readers what they are like by their actions.

to release a new book. Issues like these, however, can render your introduction redundant.

Third, writing a good intro can be the hardest part of a non-fiction book. You need to lay out the scope of what is ahead and say what the reader will gain from reading your book. It also needs to be engaging and accurate. It's far easier to complete this task with the full knowledge of your book's content in your head – as opposed to basing it on what you *think* you will write in due course. With the full scope of the book in mind, your introduction will flow more easily and be far more effective.

Leave your introduction for later and begin with chapter one.

Have goals

With writing, as with any task, it's good to set yourself goals. Goals are helpful markers on the journey and you feel good when you achieve them. Our tip is to set yourself a realistic target for each day. If you're working on a 100-page tuition book, if you can manage to write 3-4 pages per day, you'll have hit your target in one month. If you're writing a 30,000 word self-help book, you could aim to produce 1,500 words per day, and in 20 days you'll be done.

The key is to make the target achievable. If you say to yourself, "Today I'm going to nail this and write 5,000 words," but only manage 2,000 words, you'll feel like you failed. (Even though writing 2,000 good words a day is a target for many full time writers). Consistently miss your goals and you'll end up feeling miserable. If, however, your target is 1,000 words per day and you produce 2,000, you'll feel like you're majorly winning.

Find your rhythm and pace yourself. We would advise against writing all day, even if the opportunity arises. Beyond 10 or so sides of A4 you will probably burn out, or there will be a noticeable drop off in quality. Better to write 7-8 sides of high quality material and down tools for the day to go and do something else. Your future self will thank you.

As we tire, we become less objective about our work and sometimes don't recognise when we're getting tired. After a long day of writing it's easy to make mistakes, and you'll waste time later fixing them. When we complete our part of writing a book, we know we will be passing the text onto various freelancers to do their part (copyediting, proofing, interior design etc.), so making mistakes can have ramifications down the line, including costly delays.

Pacing ourselves pays dividends, because the finished work is in a much better state when others receive it to do their bit, and the production process becomes more streamlined and efficient.

Working to a paced schedule like this has enabled Joseph to write and publish one book per month, spend a few weeks promoting it, rest for a couple of weeks, then start the process again. We know that each new title Fundamental Changes releases earns, on average, $600 per month on an ongoing basis (although some make a lot more and a few make a lot less), so it makes sense to invest some money using freelancers to speed up publication.

As an aside, you should only use freelancers once you fully understand the whole publishing process and have identified the tasks that fall outside of your skill set. We'll discuss the area of getting freelance help in more detail in a later chapter.

While writing, keep writing

Focus on getting all you want to say down on paper. At this stage, don't get bogged down with formatting your book – that task can be performed later. It's important to feel that you are always moving forward and making progress. While we always aim for excellence when writing, we know that editing what has been written is a necessary task. Tweaks can and will happen, but they can happen later. For now, it's important to capture your ideas while they are fresh.

If you know you need to include a reference, just insert <*ref*> in the text for now and find the information later. Otherwise, an Internet search will turn into checking Facebook, and maybe Twitter, and … you get the picture. It's very easy to get distracted when you're writing.

Even a basic fact-hunt can take you way off piste. If you know you're making sense, keep going!

When you're writing, keep writing. Try not to keep going back over your work and re-wording it. This will come later. The writing phase is for writing. The revision stage is for editing and corrections. Stay focused.

Don't aim for perfection in your first draft

Many writers suffer from analysis paralysis – a condition where they won't progress with their writing until they believe everything is perfect. In practical terms this means they will go over and over sentences and paragraphs, drafting and redrafting until they feel they can move on.

Read this sentence twice: "You have permission to make mistakes and get it wrong."

We met with a potential author whose internal monologue was preventing him from writing at all. Despite being a very well-spoken chap, the little voice in his head was telling him he was "stupid and dumb" if he couldn't write a well-crafted sentence or got his punctuation wrong. Because of this niggling doubt he'd never sat down to write what could have been a great series of books.

Allow us a short rant here…

It's good to strive for excellence in your work, but when you're drafting your book, the truth is most people won't notice an out-of-place comma. Your word processor will let you know about 90% of your mistakes, and proof-reading plugins like Grammarly are incredibly smart.

When we were children, we made mistakes all the time when learning new things. There was a time when we all messed up the alphabet, spelt our names wrong and didn't know where a full stop went. However, because we were expected to make errors, and they were hopefully corrected in a friendly and constructive way, we learned and got better.

At a certain point though, people may have started to call us out on our errors, embarrass us, or imply that learning is something only children do. There's a common perception that learning stops at college, university, or when we get a job. This is actually quite damaging to us psychologically, because we become reluctant to try new things. The truth is that the people who most inspire us are normally the ones who continue to learn, explore and develop as humans.

As the cliché goes, it took Edison over 2,000 attempts to create his lightbulb. He didn't see this as 2,000 failures, he saw it as discovering 2,000 ways *not* to make a lightbulb. If he'd given up (or never started) because he didn't know how to do something, he'd never have got there.

In our experience, it's easy to get hung up on the "theory" rather than the "practice". It's easy to become obsessed with the *art* of writing to the point where the story gets lost, or the point of your writing is obscured.

In Fundamental Changes, we could get bogged down in music theory and spend too much time discussing the *why* instead of focusing on the *how*. One thing Joseph always told his guitar students was that music was made first and theory came afterwards. Music theory is simply a way of explaining what has happened – a way of reverse engineering what people have played so that other people can play it and discover why it sounds the way it does. But what began as a noble endeavour (normally by people with leather patches on the elbows of their cardigans) became a dogma – a set of rules never to be broken.

In one sense, it's extremely useful to have a set of rules to work within, in order to create something, but in another sense it's really bad. Why? Because it can stifle creativity. It's damaging to tell a music student, "These are the rules. If you don't follow them you are making BAD music!" Just as it's damaging to tell a writer, "If you don't abide by the rules and get everything perfect you are creating BAD literature!"

The fact is, virtually every advancement in the field of arts and entertainment has been made by disruptors who saw things differently and decided to push the boundaries of what was "safe" – or just worked completely outside of the box.

As well as literature, the same applies to photography, dance, acting etc. We each have our own voice. The visionaries who push the boundaries of a discipline are the ones we remember. Hendrix, Murakami, van Gogh, Ansel Adams, Scorsese…

All that to say, let's get our hands dirty and *just write*! Get your ideas out. Tim recalls working with one author who pointed at a graveyard and commented, "Do you know what that is? Lost potential. Thousands of unwritten books."

We may not be writing *The Brothers Karamazov* or *A Brief History of Time*, but we do know that the collective books we've produced have helped thousands of people to enhance and improve their lives in numerous ways. That's enough for us. We don't need to be famous, but we do want to be effective. Let's not be afraid to get stuck in and create!

(Rant over!)

Healthy writing

Our brains are wired to focus intently for fairly short spans of time, after which we become mentally fatigued, our attention wanes and we become less effective. We're sure that the current state of the world, with the immediacy of social media, and everything delivered to us in bite-size chunks, has eroded our attention spans even more.

Writing is a solitary pursuit and is usually done sitting down, so be kind to yourself. Take a short break every 15 minutes and stretch or walk around. Every hour, leave your writing space and get a drink (ideally something without caffeine so you won't become dehydrated, although there are those days when writing is tough and nothing but a strong coffee will suffice!)

The human body isn't really designed for sitting and most of the little niggles we have in our bodies are from sitting for too long. There are plenty of studies showing that sitting for long periods can cause serious mobility issues in later life.

You could purchase a standing desk or make your own. At a minimum, research the correct screen and keyboard heights for someone your size and ensure that your working environment is as ergonomic as possible. Make sure everything is comfortable *for you*.

Go out for a walk too, or engage in some other form of exercise. Getting some fresh air and spending half an hour walking can help to clear the mind and generate fresh inspiration. It can provide the perspective you need to solve the problem you've been grappling with. Tim goes swimming several times a week and goes for an evening walk. Joseph walks his dogs, goes for strength and conditioning sessions at his local gym several times per week and also has one-on-one boxing training.

While we're writing this, we're also painfully aware that this is the advice you're most likely to ignore, but don't! If you keep yourself fit and healthy you'll feel better and be more productive. Both of us have previously suffered from, "I haven't got time to do that, I've got too much work to get done" syndrome. But we've both had the epiphany that when we put our lifestyle above our work, we feel so much better about ourselves, and we get just as much work done as before... but enjoy it more!

Long working hours does not equal increased productivity. Effective working hours equals productivity. And more productivity = more books = more success.

As well as exercise, diet plays a huge role in productivity. It's easy to have a packet of biscuits or crisps (cookies and chips across the pond) open on the desk next to you. These are the worst kinds of fuel for your body. They're just empty calories that don't help your body work. Eat fruit, nuts and clean, unprocessed foods. Drink water (unfortunately we're both English, so we drink a lot of tea). Good decisions about food and exercise improve your life, not just your writing.

Try not to stay up too late writing unless you're a night owl and your social situation means you can have a commensurate lie-in the next day. Quality of sleep is as important as good exercise and nutrition.

The moral of this story is simple. Look after yourself and you'll write better books.

Dealing with writer's block

We rarely get writer's block. Sorry, we know. How annoying! But there are reasons for this that we'd like to share, because they might help you.

Joseph:
I know what I need to write because I plan out each book before I write it. With the detailed plan in front of me, if I get stuck on one chapter, I can stop working on it and jump into another. By the time I've finished this new section, my ideas have usually subconsciously sorted themselves out and I'm able to conquer my initial stumbling block.

I break all my content into clear sections and aim to pack in as much information as I can (these tend to be 3-4 pages long). As previously mentioned, I don't worry about writing too much and inevitably I end up with the section being too long. If this happens frequently then my circa 100-page book might end up with 40 extra pages. Rather than edit this material down, deleting stuff, I take out anything that doesn't need to go in this book and put it to one side. In due course I'll repurpose that material for a new book. Working like this means that a book that was planned as a single title often happily gets an unplanned sequel. (I still love them, though, even if they were unplanned!)

Granted, I'm not writing fiction, so I don't get stuck trying to develop plots or characters. I'm simply writing down what's in my head as I would explain it to a student. This really makes writing quite simple for me as everything I do is practical and (hopefully!) fact-based. Sharing my knowledge and expertise is obviously a lot easier than creating a fantasy universe.

If you do write fiction, it occurs to me that you should probably keep writing, even though you might not like what you're saying. As a musician, I've done plenty of gigs where I felt my playing was terrible, only to be approached afterwards by people who really loved my stuff. Your writing could very well be better than you think. Keep going because you can always rewrite it later. No one will know.

Tim:

Elie Wiesel, the holocaust survivor and author of many books including the bestselling *Night*, spoke about how he personally grappled with his writing:

"Acutely aware of the poverty of my means, language became obstacle. At every page I thought, 'That's not it.' So, I began again with other verbs and other images. No, that wasn't it either. But what exactly was that *it* I was searching for?"

But he kept going, kept labouring at the coal face until he unearthed what he was looking for.

After ghosting around 30 books for other people, the biggest lesson I've learned is that writing is a small bit of inspiration and a large chunk of workmanlike, diligent craft.

Today, you may get up and feel less than inspired to write. Any number of factors could mitigate your work: you had a row last night with your partner and the air still hasn't cleared; you've got a bit of a cold; you're tired, etc.

I advise you not to wait for the perfect storm of free time and inspiration to strike. Sit down now and write something. Keep chipping away at it and get those ideas out. The very act of writing will bring the inspiration you're lacking. You may feel as though you are hacking away with a blunt instrument for a while, but suddenly, it's there. You catch a glimpse of what you really want to say and how you want to say it.

In the words of Stephen King, "If you want to be a writer, you must do two things above all others: read a lot and write a lot. There's no way around these two things that I'm aware of, no shortcut" and "Amateurs sit and wait for inspiration, the rest of us just get up and go to work."

Book titles and subtitles

We turn to the topic of your book title last, which in our opinion is the right time to address it – after you've written it. Naming your book before you start writing, although tempting, creates more problems than it solves – not least because you may find yourself making a thousand tiny compromises when you write ("Yes, but I can't say that because my book is called X.") Your book title is one of the most important tools you have to sell it, so here is our advice on titles and subtitles:

Joseph:
There is an art to naming a non-fiction book, and if you do it right you'll create a vital tool that will help your book get discovered by the right audience. My book titles are descriptive and very boring! Each book is named to describe exactly the content it includes. Examples include,

- Complete Technique for Modern Guitar
- The Practical Guide to Modern Music Theory for Guitar
- The Complete Guide to Playing Blues Guitar
- Chord Tone Soloing for Jazz Guitar
- Rock Rhythm Guitar Playing
- Beginner's Guitar: The Complete Guide
- Fingerstyle Blues Guitar

They may not sound exciting, but each one describes its content accurately. More importantly, the titles work well because people searching for products on Amazon will type in search terms such as, "Guitar Technique", "Theory for Guitar", "Play Blues Guitar" "Jazz Guitar Soloing", etc.

I'm very careful not to "keyword spam", as that is against Amazon's terms of service, but I also use relevant terms in the subtitle of my book. For example:

Guitar: *The Circle of Fifths for Guitarists: Learn and Apply Music Theory for Guitar*

Guitar Chords in Context: *Learn to Construct and Apply Essential Guitar Chords*

Guitar: The First 100 Chords for Guitar: *How to Learn and Play Guitar Chords, the Complete Beginner Guitar Method*

These subtitles go a step further in accurately describing the content and who the book is targeted at. They too contain many useful keywords that people will be searching for. The right title and subtitle combination will help your book to be found – it's as simple as that.

Tim:

I wasn't far into my publishing career when I discovered that authors have a penchant for esoteric book titles. And soon after that I discovered that the book buying public doesn't do cryptic (maybe in fiction, granted, but definitely not in non-fiction).

The main problem with cryptic titles is that the phrase the author has plucked out of the ether only means something to them. Others may well get it, but not until they've read the book. It's a nice idea, but actually, the person you want to capture is the casual bookshop or online browser; the potential customer who spots your book and says, "Hey, that's exactly what I'm looking for."

Whenever I've called out an author for wanting a baffling book title, they have invariably countered with,

"Yes, but I have this subtitle to explain it."

My reasoning is, if you need a subtitle to explain your main title, then the subtitle should *be* the main title. Simple as that. Why make it difficult for people to get what your book is about?

* * *

Remember: don't stuff your title/subtitle with keywords, but choose words that legitimately describe the content of your book that people will be searching for. These words should occur naturally in a book's product description. This will reinforce the search terms and help potential customers find your books easily. We will talk about building the perfect product description in a later chapter.

Remember: Think about the content of your book and what potential customers will be searching for when you name it. Keep your titles relevant to the content and don't lie to get search results.

For example, if your book is about Italian cooking, don't use the word "Chinese" because you think it'll produce more results. It is unlikely that someone searching for a Chinese cookery book will buy your Italian cookbook anyway, so it really is a waste of time. Go and write a Chinese cookbook instead!

Title writing strikes a balance between Search Engine Optimisation (SEO) and describing your book in the best possible light. Once your book is on Amazon, it will show up in a Google search, so anything you can do to make your books search friendly will get potential customers to your sales page.

There are countless books occupying every niche imaginable, so for a reader to find the book you've written is like them looking for a needle in a haystack (except they don't even know there is a needle in there). They are much more likely to search for something they want by subject matter than title. Careful titling will help them to find you.

Incidentally, we try not to name our books, "Jazz Book 1", "Jazz Book 2", etc. We've found to our cost that people tend to avoid buying book three in a series because they think they need to have mastered the two previous volumes first. Make each book a standalone volume. The movie *The Madness of George III* had to be re-titled because the studio thought audiences wouldn't watch it before seeing The Madness of George I and II!

Chapter Four: Writing Tools and Formatting Your Book

Now we move into very practical territory. The chapters that follow cover every aspect of the publishing process, including how to launch and market your book effectively and more. But first, we asked a Facebook writers' forum what they would like to see included in this book and a surprisingly high number of the responses wanted to know about writing tools and formatting, so we'll address that issue now.

We live in a world where our Internet history is constantly tracked and we are served up adverts based on what we look at. We find ourselves in an echo chamber that supports our own views. If we search for wooden ladders, the Internet will try to sell us all the varieties of wooden ladder known to man. Why are we telling you this? Because the Internet knows you're a writer. To that end, Facebook and Google will attempt to serve you hundreds of ads to sell you writing productivity apps, writing coaching courses, and publishing marketing success strategies.

Some of the resources might be awesome, but you can begin to create your book with very simple tools without it costing a lot of money.

The writing / productivity tools we use are:
• Pens and notepads for quickly recording ideas
• Mac desktops, and MacBooks for when we're travelling or doing poor work in front of the TV
• Microsoft Word (which works better with Kindle Direct Publishing than the Pages app)
• Music notation software (specific to Fundamental Changes)
• The "Notes" software on Mac for making lists and crossing things off when they're done (or a simple paper list)
• Adobe Photoshop to edit images and design front covers
• Adobe InDesign for producing internal book layouts

That's it. We've moved to using Photoshop and InDesign because they are top end, professional publishing tools and (once the learning curve has been crested) they can massively speed up your workflow. However, you don't necessarily need to invest in these tools and there are cheaper or free alternatives. These might not give you as much power or control, but if your work isn't super complicated, they can get the job done perfectly well.

Apart from that, we try to work smart. We try not to waste time doing things that could be automated in some way. If we need to process lots of images, we'll create a simple action in Photoshop to process them as a batch. It's possible to click one button and have an action format your cover into the different sizes required for your website i.e. Kindle, iBooks or PDF. If there are things in Word we find ourselves doing often, we'll create keyboard shortcuts to do them. Automating tasks is cool and a huge timesaver.

Consistency

Joseph:

I have found that writing multiple books is the best way to get discovered, build a brand, and develop confidence and trust in my readers. However, when I first started writing I just put information on paper and tried to get my teaching across as best I could.

I've been lucky in life and I'm very fortunate that my brother is a professional editor of scientific journals. He definitely got the brains! In the early days he very kindly checked all of my books and spent time on Skype going through every single correction.

After reading about four of my books he made a general observation that there was a lack of consistency in my terminology and formatting from one book to another. Here's an example of the sort of conundrum I was dealing with:

When playing the guitar, we name the fingers of the fretting hand 1, 2, 3 and 4. There are 4 beats in a bar of music. There may be 4 or more bars in a section of music. On the guitar neck, the frets are numbered from 1 to 24. The strings are numbered from 1 to 6.

Bearing this in mind, it's possible to have sentences like this:

"Use the 2nd finger to play the 4th fret on the 3rd string in the 3rd beat of the 2nd bar."

At first glance this sentence is not easy to read, and if something has to be read really slowly to be understood then it's not right. Based on my brother's advice I combined ordinal and cardinal numbers with a sensible grammatical structure and created a set of rules that I could use myself and teach to other authors – with the purpose of clarifying the content for the reader. In my books,

- Beats are always 1st, 2nd, 3rd, etc.
- Bars are always first, second, third, etc.
- Fingers are always first, second, third, etc.
- Frets are always 1st, 2nd, 3rd, etc.

Our house style now dictates that the above example be rewritten:

"On the 3rd beat of the second bar, use your second finger to play the 4th fret on the third string."

It's instantly more readable and the reader isn't being bombarded with numbers.

This example is specific to my subject matter, but the point is that developing consistency helps readers to quickly recognise and understand your message.

Tim:

Paying attention to consistency in how your text is formatted might seem like a pedantic thing, but actually serves a very important purpose.

First, applying formatting consistently helps the reader to understand how your book is organised and what each section means. E.g. the use of italics, or a different font, or some kind of simple separator can signal to the reader that the main part of the chapter has come to an end and they are now in the conclusion or reflection section.

Subheadings (usually called A headings by publishers) can be incredibly useful roadmaps for the reader that tell them, "This is where we're going" or "This is where we are now". It's important to use different formatting for any headings that come under the subheadings (usually called B headings), so that it is clear and obvious what they are. All of this helps you to deliver the information to the reader in a structured manner and helps them to process it more easily.

As well as vastly improving readability, having consistent formatting will give your books a consistent look and feel, and this is helpful in building a cohesive brand where people know what to expect.

* * *

Here are a few other basic points of style that we ask authors of non-fiction tuition books to observe:

- Write with authority. Your reader has paid for your book. They are happy to accept that you are a subject matter expert unless you tell them otherwise. For this reason, state the facts and show people what to do

- Don't start sentences with, "Next, I want you to *try* to do this…". Worse still, "If you *want*, you can *try* to do this." As Yoda said, "Do or do not, there is no try!" Instead, simply tell people what to do in clear terms. Better to write, "This next example shows you how to…" and "Complete the next task by doing…"

- Try not to say "I" too much unless you are genuinely sharing a personal opinion or experience

- Avoid verbose passages of prose that don't actually say much or add any value to your message. Don't use three words if one will suffice

- Keep to the one idea per sentence rule and strive to make your sentences clear and easily understood. It's so easy to fall into the trap of writing convoluted sentences. You may know what you mean, but others may find it frustrating or impenetrable. Here's an example from a book Tim edited recently.

Original sentence: "For a moment see if you can close your eyes and think of an early memory of a moment where you felt happy or excited."

Edited sentence: "Close your eyes for a moment and see if you can think of an early memory where you felt happy or excited."

Notice that the original a) had no punctuation, b) repeated the word "memory" and c) essentially asked the reader to try and see if they could close their eyes. The "trying" part was meant to relate to the memory rather than the eyes.

It's fine to have a style as a writer – your style can help people connect with you and your topic – but be consistent with it. Don't flit between gossip columnist and neurosurgeon.

Formatting while writing

We've discussed how we consciously use chapters, subheadings, short paragraphs and simple language to make our books easy to write and understand. Now let's discuss how to use text styles and formatting in your document. We are making two assumptions here:

1. That you'll be using Microsoft Word for writing and formatting. Apologies to anyone who is not, but our guess is that most are.

2. That in due course you will publish your book via Kindle Direct Publishing (KDP) in Kindle eBook format as well as paperback. There are certain ways of formatting your document in Word that, if observed, will make this process go much more smoothly.

We have developed a Word master template with specially formatted styles that we use for each book we produce. The headings and body text styles have been designed to convert perfectly to Kindle when the Word document is uploaded to KDP. You can download this template from **www.self-published.co.uk.** Head to the website and get it now. **(http://geni.us/authordownloads)**

Headings

In the template, you'll see that we use three separate heading styles and that, initially, everything is formatted in Times New Roman. Later, Kindle readers can choose the font they prefer to read with.

Heading styles are incredibly important because the index page of the Kindle book is automatically generated using them.

The headings indicate a nested hierarchy of sections (kind of like Russian dolls).

Heading 1 is used for the main "top-level" chapter titles

Heading 2 sits beneath that and represents main headings (A headings) within a chapter. These represent the different sections/topics covered in each chapter

Heading 3 is used for subtopics (B headings) that sit under the sections above

Heading 1 (Chapter)
Text goes here.
   Heading 2 (Subtopic)
   Text goes here.
      Heading 3
      Text goes here.
   Heading 2
   Text goes here.
      Heading 3
      Text goes here.
      Heading 3
      Text goes here.

Always use Heading 1 for chapter titles and Heading 2 for subheadings. Flip back to the contents page of this book and you'll see how this translates into an index. We can't stress enough how important it is to use headings. Not only do they help you and your readers to navigate your work, but they generate the table of contents (TOC) vital to the successful formatting of the digital edition of your book.

When you submit your work to KDP, your document will be rejected if the TOC isn't set up correctly, so it's worth taking the time to understand how this works.

The headings below have been created with heading styles:

This is a Heading 1 Style

This is a Heading 2 Style

This is a heading 3 Style

To apply a heading style, type your text (for example the chapter title), select it, and from the "Home" menu in Word, click Heading 1 or Heading 2, etc.

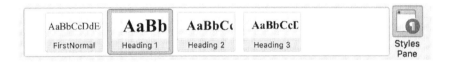

If you need to spend more time on this, there are plenty of good articles on the Internet. Google "how to use heading styles in Word" for more information.

Fonts

People often ask us about fonts. Writers can get hung up on this sort of thing. Tim recalls one author specifying that he wanted his book laid out using one specific font. It wasn't a nice font to work with (in terms of its natural spacing), and it wasn't very readable either! At the end of the day, there is a reason why so many books are set in Times, Garamond and other basic fonts. They just work and are easy on the eye.

Generally, when working with text for eBooks, we just use bog-standard Times New Roman. This might sound a bit boring, but it's perfect for the transition to Kindle. You may want to spend more time thinking about and experimenting with fonts for the printed version of your book. If so, there are plenty of beautiful royalty-free fonts out there you can use (such as at **www.dafont.com** for instance).

A Kindle, however, can only display a limited number of fonts and the chances are your reader will already have a favourite. Once your book has been processed by KDP on upload, it is no longer stored as "words" as such, but data, in a reflowable text format. Using a simple font like Times New Roman allows your reader to decide how they would like your book to appear on their screen.

This applies to font sizes too. Authors will sometimes use a bigger font in their Word document for dramatic effect, but on Kindle this will just be displayed at whatever size the reader chooses, so it's better to use bold or italics for emphasis instead.

Body Text

It's important to use a text style for your main body text as well as your headings. Every piece of text that is not a heading needs to be properly formatted. If you've downloaded the Word template from our website, you'll see a text style called "FirstNormal". (Go to **http://geni.us/ authordownloads**) We use this style for all body text in our books. Once again, the font is Times New Roman, but we've pre-formatted it to have the correct spacing for Kindle.

You can universally change any aspect of a style or heading just by clicking a few buttons. For example, if you want to change the font, size, line spacing, colour, margins etc., of FirstNormal, all in one go, this can be achieved easily from the Styles Pane in Word.

The icon that opens the Styles Pane is located at the far right when the "Home" tab is selected. Click on the icon to expand the pane and work with the different styles.

Alternatively, you can simply *right click* the style you want to edit in the Home tab. A sub-menu will appear. Select "Modify".

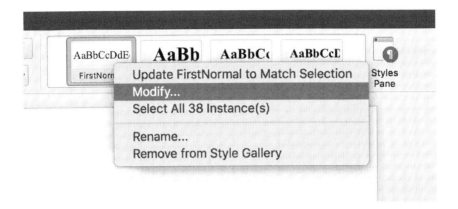

This will open the following dialogue box where you can view and change the various settings for the style:

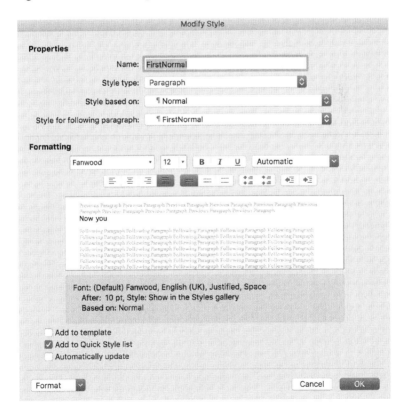

Tip: if you decide at some point to create your own text styles, checking the box "Add to Quick Style list" will add them to the "styles gallery". This refers to the style shortcut icons that appear on the Home tab as illustrated above.

Backing-up and redundancy

When we're writing or editing, we don't initially store documents on our local computers. Instead we work in the Cloud and any copies of documents on our Macs are for backup purposes. Working this way means we can hop from desktops to laptops and the files we're working on are automatically synchronised, so we're always certain to be working on the latest version.

We decided that Dropbox best suited our purposes. It synchronises files easily with its desktop app and it also makes it easy for collaborative working on documents. A free Dropbox Basic account will give you 2GB of space, which is plenty for most people. There are three other subscription options for those who need more space (1TB and 2TB options), but it's unlikely you'll need such a large amount of storage.

There are, of course, other ways of working in the Cloud and collaborating on documents, such as Google docs and One Drive, and you may have your own preferences.

Any documents we are working on right now are saved to a Dropbox folder and, at the end of each writing session we'll save a backup copy on our Macs. At the end of each day, we'll also save an additional copy of the file to a different Cloud storage folder. This gives us two backups in different locations, should the unthinkable happen and our Macs blow up and Dropbox goes down, all on the same day. If a global cataclysm wipes out all three copies of our document, well we'll probably have more pressing matters to attend to in any case, such as digging fallout shelters in our cellars and stockpiling cans of beans.

As if all of this wasn't enough, once a month we back up all our work to portable hard drives which we store in super-secret places that no one knows about.

Organisation goes hand-in-hand with backing up and is not a problem if you are only working on one book, but we now have over 100 books in our catalogue (excluding various foreign language translations), so we need to maintain a consistent filing system in Dropbox. Ours looks like this:

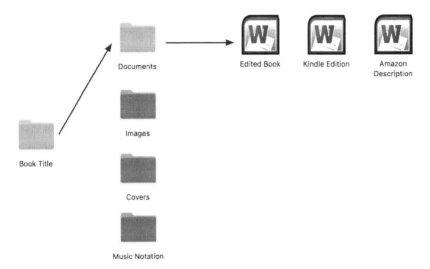

Inside the main book folder we have subfolders separating the project into distinct areas:

1. Documents (the master edited version of the book; the Kindle formatted version; our Amazon product description).

2. Images (any images used in the book).

3. Cover design files (Photoshop master document, any stock photography images etc).

4. Music notation files (PDFs and prepped images).

We also add shortcuts to our Finder menu (the Mac equivalent of what used to be called Windows' File Manager – now File Explorer). For example, there is a shortcut to the main books folder, one to other authors' files, one to front cover designs, etc. This makes it quick and easy to find what we need. There's nothing worse than having an idea in your head that you can't get down because you can't quickly locate the document you need.

Using images

Images can be tricky things to work with in both digital and physical publishing.

The most important thing to remember is that any image you import into your document must have been created at a resolution of 300dpi (dots per inch). This is the standard for professional print and will achieve good results. It's entirely possible to print using images of a lower resolution, but they won't look sharp and well-defined.

If you are supporting your book with images or diagrams, make sure that you are free to use the image without infringing anyone else's copyright. A common misconception here is that if you find an image through a search on Google images, and it doesn't have the © symbol, or any wording plastered across it, then it must be free to use – because it's in the public domain, right? Wrong! Just because an image hasn't been watermarked does not mean it's free to use and you could fall foul of a lawsuit. If you are able to track down the photographer who created the image, you must seek and receive their permission before publishing the image. This applies whether you want to use an image for a cover design or inside your book.

If you're not in a position to create your own images/diagrams, then what resources are available?

There are a number of "free" image websites that have a limited number of images to use. Usually, these sites exist as a loss leader for bigger companies who sell hundreds of thousands of images. Be careful though, even these free images are given under license and they are not always free for commercial use. **https://pixabay. com** is a good site with lots of free images that *are* in fact free for commercial use.

Alternately, you would need to turn to one of the large, royalty-free stock photography sites to buy the images you need. Shutterstock, Fotolia, Canstock Photo and 500px are all good options. Between them they host millions of images. Depending on the size you're after, these images can be expensive, but you'll be properly licensed to use the image for your book cover or inside your book, and the images are so good that they are beyond the photographic capabilities of most of us mortals.

Despite so many images being available, however, sometimes you need something so specific that the only option is to create it from scratch. If we need anything bespoke creating, our first port of call is normally **www.upwork.com.** On Upwork you will almost certainly find a designer who can meet your needs and who will work for a reasonable fee. There are some very talented artists around the world and we find that South East Asia and The Philippines are great places to start.

One piece of important advice we'd like to pass on is *do not use your word processor to edit your images!* In fact, we can't stress this enough. As good as Word is, it's not professional image editing software and it can corrupt the dpi (dots per inch) resolution of your images if you mess about with them. Also, Word is sneaky! For example, if you tell it to display an image as black and white, it will do just that – *display* it in black and white – but it will store it in your document as colour and this will cause you problems later.

The most we will ever do to an image in Word is resize it, but we don't do this by grabbing the corners of the image and dragging. Instead, we perform this task by right-clicking on the image and choosing "Size and Position":

In the resulting dialogue box you can type in the exact dimensions you require for the image.

Also to be avoided like the plague is copying and pasting images into Word (or dragging them from your desktop). This will normally result in the image being displayed at 72dpi – which is far too low a resolution for print and not acceptable to the KDP algorithms that process your file. When adding an image to your document, be sure to use the Insert – Pictures – Picture from File command:

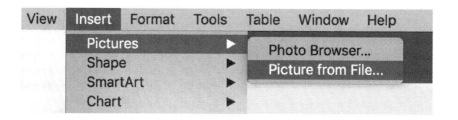

This is a safe method for adding images to Word which will ensure they remain at their original, high resolution. When adding lots of images, we create a keyboard shortcut for this command.

Since the ultimate destination for this file is Kindle, don't get too creative with where you place your images, because Kindle can't process clever text or image boxes. Keep things simple and place your images "in-line" between paragraphs of text with a clear line space either side. Having a hard return before and after an image means that readers will be able to tap on the image and enlarge it on their Kindle.

In summary…

• Use 300dpi images

• Use the Insert menu to add your images; don't paste them into Word

• Don't edit your images in Word apart from resizing them from the Size and Position menu

• Images should be placed "in line" with no text wrapping

• Leave a blank line both before and after your image

Now that we've discussed the writing process and some basic considerations of formatting your book, we will turn to the topic of adding value to your work. This is a vital component of the publishing process and, if you get it right, is the one factor that will help build your brand as an author more than any other.

Chapter Five: Content and Adding Value

First things last

So far we have covered in detail the process of planning, organising and writing your book. We are non-fiction publishers, so the bulk of our examples stem from that kind of publishing, but we've endeavoured to keep things fairly broad and think in terms of *principles*. Now we address a very important factor that goes to the heart of a successful publishing strategy: *adding value*. We'll talk about how we do this with our type of book, but you can do the same, regardless of the type of book you're publishing – even fiction.

Engage the reader

Your first job as an author is to make sure you engage the reader with your content. Someone has spent their hard-earned cash on your book, so they want (and expect) it to be good. They actually want you to succeed in teaching them about the subject they love.

Feel free to show them your passion for your topic and your expertise in talking about it, but also guide them by the hand. We advocate a layer upon layer approach to non-fiction books. Don't go in with all guns blazing then spend the rest of the book trying to explain why you said what you said. Start small and build. Take things in logical, incremental steps.

In our music tuition books, the first examples we show the reader are always easily manageable, which means they get an immediate pay off. If you're writing a book on Yoga or meditation, make your first exercises super simple but effective. The reader will receive positive reinforcement – "Yes! I can do this" – and their confidence will grow.

Sometimes we will write a short apology that the initial musical examples in a book are quite basic, and encourage more advanced players to skip ahead if needs be. Pretty much any guitarist can play those early examples, but we want to write with an inclusive attitude. Just a few pages later the examples will be harder. We guide the reader from a simple starting point to engage in a journey that will result in them mastering a particular style in all its complexity. Whatever you are writing about, guide the reader, step by step.

The golden rule in fiction writing is "show, don't tell". This is equally applicable to non-fiction, especially if you are teaching the reader something new. You may not think you are writing an instructional book, but all reading is learning, so by default, you are teaching.

Don't try to be smart, wielding your knowledge like a club! Don't blind them with science. Your attitude as a writer should be, "I'm fortunate enough to have walked this journey before. Let me show you the way." People can relate to that and connect with you.

If you attend a gym, you'll probably recall your first day there was a bit daunting. You're not sure what to do, you don't know anyone, and it's embarrassing to ask. Normally, though, long time members are only too happy to show you what's what. But, there is always that one arrogant guy who turns up his nose at the newbies, right? He's a bit patronising and instead of offering advice, sighs and tuts over your ignorance. Don't be that guy. No one likes that guy.

We've said earlier that when you write, do so with authority. Someone has bought your book and, as far as they are concerned, you are a subject expert. Let's qualify that by saying you should assume the role of "expert and eager helper". Don't be self-effacing – you're an expert – but don't shove information down people's throats or patronise them either.

The weirdest tip we can give you in this book is to smile when you write! You'll be instantly lifted and this will reflect in your work. You'll also get attractive smile lines. Bonus!

The most important success secret we can give you

Perhaps the most important thing we can teach you is to include something of genuine value in your book – something that will enhance the reader's experience and leave them feeling satisfied. The mantra of an American publishing colleague of ours is, "What's the takeaway?" They aren't hankering after noodles or fried chicken, they just want every book they publish to gives the reader something tangible to take away.

"Added value" will vary from book to book. It could be access to bonus content such as a video interview with the author, or other VIP goodies. It could be a downloadable study guide or similar resource. If you've written a business book it could be access to free templates, a business plan, or financial forecasting tools. However you do it, *add value*. We can't stress this enough.

Joseph discovered the importance of adding value accidentally by writing guitar tuition books. In fact, he would say that if he could pin his success on one thing, it was the decision to include free audio downloads with every book.

Since he was teaching music, it made sense to record high quality examples of what was being taught and make them available as MP3 files to download. It is, after all, essential for a student to hear what they are supposed to sound like. Publishing via KDP meant there was no way to provide a CD with a book, or embed the audio (plus, printing books with accompanying CDs is a costly business), so he created a website to host the audio, so readers could easily download it.

As he wrote successive books, he could see that the audio download page on his website was getting more and more hits. The readers' experience of his books was genuinely enhanced by being able to download the audio examples.

Then the penny dropped.

After reading about how email marketing was the absolute best way to sell something (it is – no question), he signed up to MailChimp and used their simple forms to ask for a reader's email address before they could download the audio to their book. MailChimp is a free (up to 2,000 addresses) mailing list provider that allows you to write and design beautiful emails and share content.

A while after this, Joseph decided to start sending free guitar lessons to those who'd signed up and a blog (which today hosts over 350 free lessons) began to take shape. People opened the emails because he wasn't selling anything and the lessons were cool and useful. Traffic on the Fundamental Changes website went up and Google noticed. This meant that the site's ranking became higher and more people found and bought the books, which meant that more people gave Joseph their email address, and the cycle continued.

The result was a growing community of happy, engaged subscribers who liked the fact that they weren't being spammed with sales offers, but were being provided with genuinely useful guitar stuff. A turning point occurred when Joseph's next book was released. A simple email to the subscriber base announced its arrival. The resulting sales were insane. That book remained in the No1 slot on the Kindle chart for weeks, meaning that it received further traction from Amazon's search algorithms.

At this point the penny dropped again: if it was possible to feed Amazon a snowball of initial sales, they would take that traffic and turn it into an avalanche. Amazon's algorithms promote what sells. If something is selling, more people will see it on Amazon.

Remember this, it is now your business strategy

We will talk more about promotion, marketing and how to engage with Amazon in later chapters, but for now, think about what kind of download you can add that would be of genuine value to your readers.

The operative words here are *genuine* and *value*. How can you enhance your book and therefore your readers' lives?

Including free audio is something we feel genuinely makes our books superior to others in the same genre. If you go to a bookshop and buy a guitar method that has audio, it will generally come with a CD or DVD. In this day and age that's old fashioned. Technology has advanced and people want MP3s they can download and drag into their music player, or stream from the Cloud. Very few publishers offer this, let alone those self-publishing via Kindle.

The moral of this tale is that by adding value we created a better product. That made customers happy. The free content helped to build a trusting relationship with our readers and yielded their email address. Today we have over 60,000 people on our mailing list and it hasn't cost us a penny to build (apart from the monthly subscription cost).

Think about that. When we launch a book, we can let 60,000 people know about it who already like our stuff. Virtually every book we release goes straight to No1 on the Amazon guitar books chart. Our titles have featured in the chart of Amazon's top 100 books across *all* genres. This has been achieved simply by adding value and building a mailing list.

MailChimp is a great way to start. Go and sign up now. It's free and an essential tool when building a list. Use the free service before you try to get fancy. Currently, Fundamental Changes uses a client called ActiveCampaign, due to the size of our database. 90% of the emails we send are automated, based on complex sets of conditions. We'll discuss email lists and automation later.

You'll have noticed that some of the bonus content for this book is available for download via our website. Yes, we'd love you to join our mailing list, but we're not simply collecting names. There are detailed guides illustrating different parts of the publishing process that will be updated regularly. Including them in the book would immediately date it. Plus, we genuinely want to add value to you, the reader, and give you stuff that will help you on your journey. We won't spam you with sales emails either. If you sign up at **www.self-published.co.uk** not only will you receive helpful tools and resources, but you'll get to see how the process of growing customer relationships via email automation works in practice. We'll even share our own templates, which you can adapt to your audience.

Think about the books you are planning to publish and how you will add value in order to build your audience. People want something truly useful in return for their email address. Don't hold back a chapter of your book that's only available online – that reduces value rather than adding it. Don't give away a crappy PDF that doesn't really enhance the content. Make it worth having. By creating a download that really matters to your readers, you immediately build trust. You enhance your brand. You develop your relationship. They think your stuff is cool, so they'll engage with your content and tell their friends. Ultimately, they will buy again.

Add value. Have integrity. This is our mantra and it needs to be yours too.

Go above and beyond what your reader is expecting.

You could provide:

- Videos
- Audio
- Images
- Templates
- An online course
- Interviews with interesting and relevant people

Diagrams and illustrations

The interior design of your book is as important as the cover, and how the interior is designed can add significant value to the content. We're lucky that we publish books that require music notation, because it fills the pages with useful information and breaks up the text, making for an easy read.

We've already discussed how the use of subheadings can break up your content into manageable and recognisable sections that provide a roadmap for the reader, and the use of diagrams and illustrations is a similarly valuable tool.

As an aside, Tim once had a difference of opinion with an author around the issue of subheadings, when editing his book and designing the interior.

"I refuse to use subheadings!" the author declared. "They are just a device to disguise sloppy writing, for authors who can't string together coherent paragraphs."

The use of subheadings was conceded, but when it came to designing the interior, the author requested clear line breaks in the text every now and again.

"Why do you want those?"

"Well, they indicate when there is a change of topic."

"I see, so what you're really asking for is blank subheadings..."

At least with a subheading the reader would have been given a heads-up regarding what was coming next!

The average Fundamental Changes book contains around 15,000 – 20,000 words and 150 diagrams. We publish in 8.5" x 11" format (close to A4), and the maximum number of diagrams we can achieve per page is 4. That's a lot of diagrams. Your book probably won't have many, but include visual information wherever you can, because it enhances the reader's experience.

We use a program called Neck Diagrams in order to illustrate musical scale patterns on the guitar neck. It's a great way of communicating a complex bit of information in a way that can be easily digested. In your book, you may decide to use an infographic to express some complex statistics, or a business methodology, or the findings of some research. The best cookbooks are those where every dish is illustrated with a beautiful photograph of what the finished meal should look like. Don't you find yourself skipping over the recipes in some books that are not accompanied by a picture? We do!

Images, whether diagrams or photographs, create much more impact than describing things in words alone. They engage the reader and give them a break from pages and pages of text. Use them whenever you can.

Introductions, conclusions, appendices and other content

Introductions should be meaningful and to the point. You might lay out the background about why you've written the book and what the reader will gain from it. How will their life be enhanced or challenged as a result of reading your book? Set out the big picture in your introduction and explain the journey you'll take together.

In Fundamental Changes books, the introduction is always followed by our "Get the Audio" page, where clear instructions are given on how to download the free content. We suggest you do something similar. Let the reader know about the added value stuff up front, and remind them as you go along. Include links here to your social media profiles and explain how readers can connect with you.

It's very important to place this page *after* the introduction. We were confused for a long time that readers constantly got in touch saying their book had not come with audio. Eventually we realised that Kindles automatically open a book to the table of contents, and our audio page was before that. We moved the location of that page and never received another complaint.

Some non-fiction writers like to write the conclusion section to their book first, in order to keep them on track and make sure their content remains on topic. We prefer to do it last, but it's really up to you. It is helpful to have a conclusion, because it's a good way of wrapping things up and reminding the reader of what you wanted them to take away from the book. It's a decisive end. Don't you hate those movies that end suddenly when you wanted to know what happened to the characters in the aftermath? That's like a book without a conclusion.

Ideally, your conclusion will summarise and reinforce the main message of your book, and give the reader a sense of satisfaction that they have learnt something and grown as a result. It's important to show them just how much they have learned, because it's often difficult to be objective about one's own progress. We often wrap up by encouraging readers to go and put into practice what they've learned right away.

Further reading, recommended listening, etc.

At the end of your book it's often helpful to include a bibliography, if you've quoted from lots of sources, and further reading recommendations. For our music books, we often include a recommended listening section that includes essential tunes in a particular style that readers ought to hear to enhance their learning. In the Kindle edition of your book, these can be hyperlinks to web pages.

Other books by the author

If you've published other titles, include a "by the same author" page and provide links to your titles. This is a golden opportunity to advertise your other books, and it's much easier to get a happy reader to buy a book than it is to acquire a new reader. We also add links to other titles in the main body of the text if the reader's experience would be genuinely enhanced by getting that other book. Don't spam readers with dozens of links to your books though. Too many Kindle books are simply adverts for the author's other work. Write a good book you can be proud of in the first place and readers will seek you out.

We have the nice problem of having a list of titles that spans two pages in full, so we edit it down to the titles that are the most relevant to the topic of the book.

Appendices

We don't often have appendices in our books, but occasionally we'll use them if we need to present a lot of information for reference that would clutter up the main body of the text. Depending on the type of book, an appendix might contain lists of other useful resources, definitions of terms, or other information that is useful, but peripheral, to the main message. In a non-fiction teaching book context, some information might be reserved for the appendix that is not immediately essential to the reader's progress.

The bottom line is: whatever you add to enhance your book, genuinely add value.

Chapter Six: Revision, Copyediting and Paid Proofing

Once you've written your book and added your introduction, conclusion, and given it an appropriate title and subtitle, it's time to take the next step in the publishing process. The first phase in that process is to finalise your text for publication. This involves giving the text a thorough edit and check through and enlisting the help of others for a third party perspective. We see the "editing" process as three distinct phases: *revision, copyediting* and *proofreading*.

Revision

After finishing the first draft of a book, it's good to create some space between you and the text before you begin editing. Take a few days off from writing and go and do something different. Listen to music; go on long walks; visit family. This gives you time to recover from the writing process and will give you the perspective to approach making any revisions to the text with a fresh mind.

Bestselling author Neil Gaiman says that he will take his book and, "read as if I've never seen it before or had anything to do with its creation. Things that are broken become very obvious suddenly."

Our revision process tends to be a reductive process whereby we rephrase, reorganise or reduce our content to make it as streamlined as possible. As Kurt Vonnegut once said, "If a sentence, no matter how excellent, does not illuminate your subject in some new and useful way, scratch it out." We will edit in bursts of 30 minutes or so, taking frequent small breaks to help us retain perspective. We will reword paragraphs to bring clarity and iron out any grammatical errors. Neil Gaiman again: "Read it as if you've never read it before. If there are things you aren't satisfied with as a reader, go in and fix them as a writer: that's revision."

We try to ensure that we are obeying our own house rules regarding style and formatting, using global searches to weed out any inconsistencies. We also look for places where we could use fewer words to clearly convey thoughts. Phrases such as "Next, I want you to consider the following example" can be whittled down to "In the following example." This is what Elmore Leonard was referring to when he said, "If it sounds like writing, I rewrite it."

Revision can involve rearranging the order of paragraphs to create a more logical flow, or even cutting whole paragraphs that, with some distance from the work, you can see are now redundant. Occasionally, we will add extra sentences if a concept we're talking about needs more explanation. Good revision is all about illuminating the message, which might mean adding more words, taking words away, or just reorganising them. We aim to streamline the book with an eye on structure, content and meaning. It's a chance to "trim the fat" to make the book a more succinct, direct experience for the reader. Once we've beaten the book into shape (which might take a day or two), it's time to move on to copyediting.

Self-Copyediting

Copyediting differs from revision in that, at this stage, you're not looking to rewrite passages, but will make small tweaks, correct inconsistencies, double check house style and iron out any typos. It's worth bearing in mind that once you've written a piece of work, then revised it, you are probably not the ideal person to copyedit your text. You'll be very good indeed if you discover more than 60% of the issues, because you're simply too close to the text and will just read over some errors without spotting them.

At Fundamental Changes we copyedit each other's work, so that a fresh pair of eyes is on it, as well as an objective perspective. You may not have this luxury, so one workaround is to print out the entire manuscript and read it with a red pen in hand. It's amazing how reading it this way (as opposed to on screen) casts it in a completely different light. Things jump out that you simply didn't see before. This process can take several hours, so it's good to do it in bursts of, say, 10 pages at a time with short breaks.

The next day is spent on the computer copying the edits from the printout into your word processor. Though this might seem laborious, reading the book in "print" helps to catch the majority of the errors we wouldn't have spotted on screen.

Even after all this, however, we're still not ready to let anyone see our manuscript.

Grammarly

We recommend investing in Grammarly Premium (**https://www. grammarly.com/premium**). It costs just under $140 per year, but it will save you that amount many times over if you write a few books. Why? Quite simply, the better shape your manuscript is in, the less work will need to be done by an editor/proof reader (or family/ friends).

If you go the route of paying a professional editor $20 per hour to read your work (editors come in all shapes and sizes and associated costs, but you generally get what you pay for), then you want them to be spotting and correcting fundamental errors, not wasting time cleaning up silly mistakes.

Grammarly is a useful step in the editing process because it will eliminate 99% of your grammatical, spelling, contextual and vocabulary issues. It will also allow you to define the style of writing you're doing and let you know the best practice for everything from academic journals, to creative non-fiction, to personal emails. Just set the style and tell Grammarly how intrusive you want it to be. For example, you may not want Grammarly to give you vocabulary enhancements.

We run our work through Grammarly at least four times. The first time we turn off all the checks apart from spelling. The next time we focus on punctuation. Then we look at contextual grammar. Finally, we look at sentence structure.

Yes, this level of detail may take an hour or two, but the results are astonishing. Grammarly also gives you the option to accept or ignore its suggestions.

A few hours work with Grammarly gets a manuscript to the level where it's finally ready for the eyes of a professional editor. The editor is happy because they're not wasting time on silly mistakes and can get their teeth into the manuscript on a deeper level. This normally means paying less for their time.

There is a free version of Grammarly too (**https://www.grammarly.com/**) if you're not ready to splash out on the full version. Your readers, reviewers, editors and bank balance will thank you.

Friends and family (trusted readers)

A "trusted reader" is anyone who is sympathetic to what you are trying to achieve, but who will read your manuscript and give you the unvarnished truth in a constructive manner.

Make sure your manuscript looks decent on screen and once you've completed the Grammarly check, print a fresh copy and make sure it's easily readable.

Feel free to say, "Aww" but Joseph generally gives his mum a copy to read once he's done with his checks. She is a great trusted reader for his books because a) she is always honest and b) is not a guitarist. If his mum can make sense of what he is telling readers to do, without any technical guitar knowledge, then the book should be fine for readers who do. His mum is under strict instructions to be as mean as possible about his writing and highlight anything that doesn't make sense to her immediately.

We stress that any readers you use to check your work should be straightforward with you. Close friends who don't want to upset you might say, "Oh, I thought it was brilliant!" which while it is nice, isn't particularly helpful. Some people will genuinely think, "Wow, you've written a book. Hats off to you. I couldn't do that" while others just don't want to tell you they think it's rubbish. Choose your sounding boards carefully!

Our strategy to combat this is to brief the readers with specifics to look for:

- Were there any parts that didn't immediately make sense to you?
- Did you spot any grammatical errors?
- In your opinion, does the book do what it promises to do?

This is more likely to result in honest, open feedback because you are inviting specific comments. If you wholeheartedly disagree with something someone says, that's OK, it's your book and you get to decide.

It's helpful to ask readers to mark up their hard copy with a coloured pen. This makes it easy to spot their comments and find things they are referring to when you're back at your word processor. We tend to consider each suggestion and then implement the ones that stand out as important. It's worth running the text through Grammarly again, because it's easy to introduce errors while writing or editing.

Paid editing and proofing

Finding an editor who both understands your work and relates to you as a person can be a challenging task, but fortunately, the Internet helps. It's a matter of hunting down the right person and this might include a couple of false starts, but there are some highly talented people out there.

Essentially, an editor will work with an electronic version of your text and make changes to it themselves – with or without tracked changes, according to your preference. Tracked changes make it easy to see and then approve/reject their changes, but it can be a pest later because it's impossible to turn off. We generally ask editors to just change the colour of any text changes to red, to make them easy to spot.

A proof reader, on the other hand, generally works from a PDF copy of your book or (if they are old school) a hard copy, which they mark up and return to you with suggested changes.

Both are doing similar jobs in that they look to highlight any typos, grammatical errors, formatting or layout errors, or bad style. A good proof reader is usually very clinical and, let's face it, a bit pedantic, but is usually a precision pair of eyes that catch anything that should not go to print.

Historically, in publishing, the tasks of copyediting, page design (or typesetting) and proof reading were all separate, clearly defined roles, but today the boundaries are blurred. Tim will perform any of these separate roles for clients, but often gets asked to do all three for ease of streamlining the process.

You may well ask yourself, after I've self-edited, run the text through Grammarly several times, and put it through trusted readers, do I *really* need to pay for a copyeditor/proofer? We say yes for two reasons: first, a really good editor/proof reader will spot stuff that everyone else has missed and it can be astonishing to see what gets picked up. Second, they will have the skillset to suggest structural improvements you won't have thought of. Third, outsourcing this task frees up your time to do other important stuff, such as creating the bonus content that will add value to your book, and designing your cover.

Once the editor/proofer's suggested corrections are returned, you can implement them and then have a final read of your book. After this, it can be considered ready for publication.

You should know, however, that even after the exhaustive process above, errors can still slip the net. With the best will in the world and a talented team around you, stuff can still sneak through. Joseph recalls having to send out apologies and free PDFs to customers when scale diagrams in a book were incorrect. Your readers will generally flag up mistakes they spot and these can be recorded in a notes document for correction later. In the age of print-on-demand, it's not the end of the world because it is possible to update interior book files online with a minimum of disruption.

Resources

Back in the day, traditional publishers were the gatekeepers to the industry. They had the monopoly on the tools and people needed to get a book to market – editors, illustrators, designers, print production

– you name it. This helped to foster the misconception that the only way to become a "proper" author was by getting signed to a publisher. Those days are long gone. Today, especially with the rise of what has been called the gig economy, there are literally thousands of freelancers with publishing skills who can help you complete your project to industry standards. Given that individuals can now publish and get direct access to the market, there is no real need to work with a publisher.

The following are our favourite portals where you can find the talent you need for a reasonable price while retaining ownership and control over your work.

Reedsy (https://reedsy.com) is a wonderful community of authors, experts and industry insiders who work together to help each other produce excellent books. Not only do they have some useful free tools for Kindle formatting, they can also put you in touch with peer-reviewed proof readers, editors, marketers and translators. Joseph was invited to join Reedsy as a marketing professional after presenting at the Amazon Academy in London in 2016. You can visit his profile here: **https://reedsy.com/joseph-alexander**

The Alliance of Independent Authors (**https://www.allianceindependentauthors.org**) is another warm community of self-published writers and professionals looking to connect. *Alli* also acts as kind of an unofficial union of self-published writers. They have great communication with Amazon and the wider industry.

Both Reedsy and Alli have a great Facebook presence, so you can go and chat to members before choosing a service.

As excellent as Reedsy and Alli are, if you're adventurous and want to save some money you can try freelancing websites such as **https://www.upwork.com** or **https://www.outsourcely.com**. We have used Upwork for image editing tasks, providing customer support, web support, and translation work.

Need some help?

If you don't want to perform every
publishing task yourself, we created,

www.self-published.co.uk

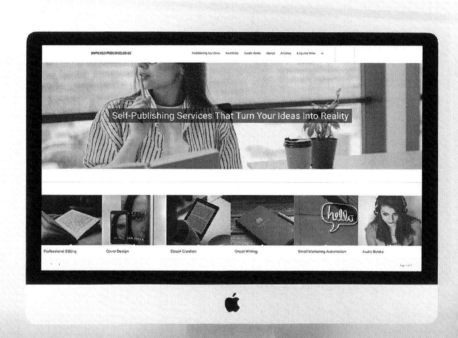

Professional services for every step
of the publishing process

Chapter Seven: Preparing your Book for Publishing

There's quite a lot of technical information in this chapter, plus you'll need to visit **https://www.self-published.co.uk/resources-for-authors/** to download the latest versions of our paperback and Kindle formatting guides. Focus on the process one step at time. Carefully following the instructions will save a lot of time and frustration later.

ISBNs

"Do I really need an ISBN?" is a question we often hear from self-publishing authors. Equal to that is the statement, "I need an ISBN, but I don't really know why. How do I get one?" There seems to be a bit of mystery and confusion about the necessity of an ISBN.

The main point of having an ISBN is so that bookshops can order your products, and the professional bodies who issue the ISBNs can track sales. If you only intend to sell your book online, then strictly speaking you don't need an ISBN, but we see them as a necessary evil in order to be taken seriously as an author and to have the opportunity of seeing your books in bookshops.

The two organisations responsible for issuing ISBNs are Bowker in the USA (**http://www.bowker.com**) and Nielsen in the UK (**http://www.nielsen.com**). It's more cost effective to buy ISBNs in batches rather than as one-offs, so if you are planning to publish more than one book, we recommend biting the bullet and buying 100 ISBNs. Warning: it is a bit expensive! As part of the process of buying the ISBNs, you will also register yourself (or your publishing imprint) with your country's provider.

At the time of writing Bowker was charging $575 for 100 ISBNs, $295 for 10, or $125 for 1. Nielsen was charging £359 for 100 ISBNs, £159 for 10, and £89 for 1.

If you are just starting out, this feels like a painful expense for something that doesn't immediately give you anything back.

Unfortunately, if you want to be taken seriously by distributors and stores, ideally you'll need to have your own official publishing identity or "imprint".

An imprint is simply a brand by which people can identify the books you publish – like having your own mini publishing house. As well as publishing your own books, in time you might publish works by other authors which complement yours. An imprint is a useful way of doing this, as the publishing industry comes to expect a certain type of book from an imprint. The imprint name can be anything you like.

The ISBNs you buy are linked to your imprint. All our ISBNs identify **www.fundamental-changes.com** as the publisher. We use our website address so that people can easily find us and to improve traffic to the site. Although it's not displayed as a link, thousands of people see it every day.

You may ask, "Do I need *100* ISBNs?" Depending on the type and quantity of books you want to publish, 10 might be sufficient, but if you get on a roll and your books are successful, you'll probably want more. We have around 100 books in our catalogue, but many have been translated into other languages, so we've used well over 200 ISBNs. Each book requires a separate ISBN for the print and digital editions, so you'll need two per book at minimum (although technically you can get away without having an ISBN for the digital edition if you're only publishing your eBook on Kindle).

Our recommendation is to take a deep breath, suck it up, and buy a pack of 100.

Free alternatives

If you're 100% certain you're only going to write one or two books, there are some free alternatives you can use.

First, there is no real requirement to add an ISBN to the digital edition of your book (Kindle, etc). When publishing via Amazon's KDP service, all your sales data is available from the seller dashboard. Similar systems are in place if you decide you want to publish digital versions with other providers, such as Kobo or Nook. The only drawback is that your sales won't be reported on by Nielsen/Bowker. If you're fine with that, then there is no need to use an ISBN on your digital edition.

For the print edition, KDP will provide you with a free ISBN and automatically register your information with **http://www. booksinprint.com** – a global database of print books maintained by Bowker. The only drawback is that your book will be categorised as "independently published" and you won't be able to connect the ISBN with your imprint name.

When Joseph began publishing he used Amazon's CreateSpace print-on-demand service – one of the biggest POD services in the world and, by necessity, perfectly integrated with Amazon's stores. Very recently, CreateSpace was absorbed into the operations of KDP, so that there is now just a single Amazon publishing platform for both print and digital. Outside of the Amazon universe, Ingram are the largest POD supplier and have options suited to both publishing companies and independent authors. For the latter, visit **https://www. ingramspark.com**. The focus of this book is publishing on Amazon, but at **www.self-published.co.uk** we'll shortly publish a guide to working with the Ingram platform.

Formatting your book for print and digital

In this book we want to show you *exactly* how to format your book. There is a different process for the print and Kindle editions. We have written detailed guides that walk you through it, step by step, highlighting the important things you need to know along the way. We've opted to provide these guides as downloadable resources from our website, because systems change and we don't want that valuable information to become redundant. We'll keep the guides up to date and notify our mailing list of any changes in the publishing process.

Head to our website now and download the PDFs. You may not be ready to act on these guides right now, but have a brief scan through them. It will help you understand everything that follows.

Formatting for paperback: http://geni.us/authordownloads
Formatting for Kindle: http://geni.us/authordownloads

Formatting for PDF

We also sell PDF versions of some books via the Fundamental Changes website, as not everyone wants to use a Kindle, or the Kindle app. A PDF version has the advantage of allowing the author to create a high-quality digital product, attract people to your website, and keep more of the profits of publishing.

There are a few minor disadvantages to selling PDF versions of your books. If you decide to enrol your digital book in KDP's Kindle Unlimited program, you can't also sell a digital version of the book elsewhere – it has to be made exclusive to KDP as long as it is in the program.

If you intend to sell your book in PDF format from your website, you will need some kind of web store facility and a payment gateway. One low cost solution is to use an ecommerce plugin (such as Woo Commerce for Wordpress) and a service like PayPal to collect the funds for a small fee. Alternatively, you can outsource the hosting and payment collection of your products to a third party.

We use Fastspring to host and sell our PDF editions (**https://fastspring.com**). As well as reducing the amount of admin required to run our website, importantly they take care of paying and reporting on the VAT that applies to PDFs. Although print books are still exempt from European VAT, unfortunately digital editions are not. (This is not a problem when selling your Kindle edition through Amazon, though, as they are the vendor and they pay the VAT).

If you do decide to sell a PDF edition of your book, you can create one very simply by importing your front cover image into your Word document as the first page, then using the "Save as PDF" option on the print dialogue screen to output your document to PDF. Go to File – Print and choose the option illustrated below.

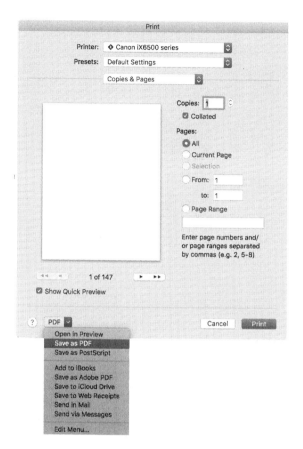

Formatting for epub

If you decide you want to try and sell your digital book on platforms beyond Kindle, then you will need to produce a copy in the ePub format. ePub is a standard for digital books that was first recognised in 2007. The idea was to create a format that would travel well between digital devices such as desktop PCs, smartphones, tablets and e-readers. Amazon decided to use their own proprietary format when they launched the Kindle.

ePub is the format you'll need if you want to publish your book via Nook (the e-reader of US bookstore giant Barnes & Noble), KOBO (a large Canadian retailer), or one of the online eBook distribution services, such as Smashwords.

With a bit of online guidance, you can use free software to convert your Word doc into ePub format. Most people recommend the open source software Calibre for this task (https://calibre-ebook.com). They have a helpful blog containing walkthroughs of the conversion process. If you don't fancy tackling this yourself, there are numerous companies online who can do the conversion for you for a modest fee.

Honourable mention: Apple Books (iBooks)

Apple Books publishes using the ePub format, but the main challenge in publishing to this platform is jumping through the hoops to do it. Formatting for Apple Books is tricky and you need to own a Mac if you want to do it yourself. Even then it's challenging. If you wrote your book using the Apple Books Author software you stand a better chance of getting a decent result.

A while ago at Fundamental Changes we paid a freelancer to convert our books to Apple Books format. At the time it was 25 books and cost $1,000. However, to date, sales via Apple Books hover around 1.5% of total sales. Kindle is so dominant in the market that it is probably not worth your time, effort or money right now. In the future things may be different.

There are plenty of digital aggregators who will help you distribute your book to a wide variety of smaller online sellers. However, we recommend uploading directly to the larger retailers (Kindle, Nook, Kobo and Apple Books).

Chapter Eight: Covers and Branding

Books are, famously, judged by their covers and you're going to need one. There are various options, but since the cover of your book is one of your most obvious and immediate selling tools, it's worth careful consideration with regard to the direction you'll take.

If you're creative and you have some digital editing skills such as Photoshop, you can have a crack at doing your own cover. But as we often say, having graphics software doesn't make you a designer, any more than standing in your garage all day makes you a car! There are some uber-talented designers out there who don't necessarily cost the earth, so you may well want to outsource this task – and it is worth doing so for the impact a great cover design will make.

One of the reasons Fundamental Changes books have been so successful is because they have a strong, easily identifiable brand image. Joseph says he accidentally discovered the branding for his books:

* * *

To cut a long story short, I can do the basics in Photoshop, but designing something from scratch is not really my forte. My original book covers were terrible: unattractive and pretty unreadable. Despite this, surprisingly they sold reasonably well. Coincidentally, after a year of writing books, my self-built website was due a makeover and it was time for a professional design makeover.

I commissioned some designers to revamp my website and, at the same time, asked them to design a Photoshop template for me that I could use to create successive book covers. The two things needed to match so that the website and book covers had a cohesive, recognisable look.

The template was fairly simple and designed in such a way that I could update the title, subtitle, author name, and the front cover image. I could then update the back cover blurb and change the overall colour scheme.

(You can view the covers at **https://www.fundamental-changes. com**).

Using this method I could create a professional looking cover in a few minutes, rather than spending ages on an amateurish-looking one. I could also do so for free, without the need to pay a designer each time.

* * *

You might think, "That's all very well, but I want each of my books to look different." Consider this, though: an unexpected benefit of the "template" approach was a growing brand recognition on Amazon. Customers could easily spot a Fundamental Changes book and often decided to buy it if it was one they hadn't seen before. Over the years that branding has become stronger and stronger as more books have been published.

As readers have a great experience with our books, they are much more likely to buy another, and by having distinct branding we make the process of recognising our books much easier for them. Combine this branding with Amazon's algorithm – "People who bought this also bought..." – and suddenly you're onto a winner. Now, when a new reader finds a book of ours on Amazon, they will also see the plethora of titles we've published, all with the same branding and all with excellent reviews.

Basic psychology tells us that if a product is seen to be popular, people are more likely to buy it. This is how big brands like Coca Cola thrive – on pre-selection. If you were shopping for a guitar method on Amazon and you clicked on one of our titles (which was surrounded by our other titles with similar branding and hundreds of five-star reviews), you would instinctively trust our book and be willing to give it a chance. Hundreds of people can't be wrong, can they? Plus, it's Amazon. If you don't like the book you can simply return it, so it's a no-lose situation.

The knock-on effects of building a brand have been huge. People read our books, hopefully enjoy them, and leave great reviews. This helps improve brand recognition and attracts new readers, who also leave good reviews, and so on... It also builds our mailing list.

Hopefully, this demonstrates why it's worth spending some money to have a great cover designed. By all means have a unique cover designed for each book you publish, but plenty of successful authors have taken a series design approach which has helped to build and reinforce their brand. If you plan to write a number of related books, then think about copying this branded approach. Check out the books by L.J. Ross (**https://www.ljrossauthor.com**) and Mark Dawson (**https://markjdawson.com**) – both are very successful, independent fiction authors who take the series design approach.

We'll say it again; good design and branding often result in exponential sales!

Branding and logos

We've discussed the fact that it's important for returning customers to instantly recognise your books. In fact, anything you can do to help people identify your work will increase your sales (as long as the content is good).

Some aspects of branding are obvious. Even consistently writing under the same name will help sellers such as Amazon to promote your book to people who have bought your titles before. I.e. if you published your first book as John Smith, stick to that. Don't switch to J.R. Smith or Johnny Smith etc. Having the same title font for your books and keeping the layout the same will further reinforce your brand. Google "Lee Child books" and you'll see what we mean. Most bestselling novelists take the same approach.

This is where the cover template approach comes into its own. You can instantly see that Lee Child's Jack Reacher books all look similar, but vary the cover image and use a different colour scheme. Apart from that, they all use the same template format.

Another aspect of branding you should consider is having someone develop a simple logo for you. Our web designers did this for us, but once again we'd suggest tapping into the talent on freelancing sites in order to gather a wide range of ideas and spend some time developing the one that is most appealing.

When Joseph realised that his books were selling well, he felt it important to register and trademark his logo to protect it around the world. This is probably not something you will need to worry about until much further down the line, so don't get hung up on it at the beginning – just write! But at some point, as you become established, you'll want to protect your brand. It's a simple process you can do online without the aid of a lawyer.

If you have a logo, use it wherever you can: on your website and on your books. If you're a non-fiction writer, have your logo on the front of your book as well as the back.

Having a logo isn't essential, but if you invest a little time in development before publishing your first book, the long-term payoff will be huge. Not only will you come across as more professional and trustworthy, you'll develop a brand that will be instantly recognisable, respected and synonymous with your genre.

Where can I get my cover designed?

There are plenty of freelance designers on the web and this can make the array of choice baffling. Cover design is one of the services we offer at Self-Published and you can view the portfolio of our recent work here: https://www.self-published.co.uk/cover-portfolio/

We offer bespoke cover designs at a very reasonable price. If your budget is super-tight, you could consider https://www.upwork.com or www.99designs.co.uk.

In short, you can get a book cover designed for anything from $50 to $500. Make sure you shop around before making your choice.

Assuming you decide to go the template/series design route, what next? The industry standard professional tool for creating and editing cover artwork is Photoshop, but this comes at a price. At the time of writing, Adobe have moved away from selling their software as a one-off package and offer a monthly Cloud subscription service. While alleviating the big, upfront cost, even a monthly subscription can seem pricey if you don't need to use the software all the time.

A perfectly reasonable alternative is a program called Gimp, which is free and open source. It will happily open Photoshop format files, and there are hundreds of online tutorials showing how to use it.

It's outside the scope of this book to teach you how to use Photoshop or Gimp (though you'll find some basic tips in the how-to videos on our website). A quick browse of **www.fundamental-changes.com** will show you how we use and adapt our design template for each of our covers, which all have the same basic layout. Occasionally, we will use a full cover image for effect and variation. We source the images from royalty free stock photography sites, such as,

www.shutterstock.com
www.istockphoto.com
www.gettyimages.co.uk
www.canstockphoto.co.uk
www.pexels.com (free)
www.stocksnap.io

If you're a dab hand with a camera, then using your own image for your book cover might be a legitimate, money-saving approach.

Once we've sourced an image we want to use, it's a matter of importing it into Photoshop and adjusting certain cover elements to suit. We often tweak the overall colour scheme to match the predominant colour in the image.

When buying images, ensure you purchase the highest resolution version possible that will fit the dimensions of your book. The smallest option will likely be too small and blowing it up to fit your book format will *decrease* its resolution and degrade the quality. Spend a few extra dollars to buy the highest quality version so that this is not an issue. We use a lot of stock imagery so we use Shutterstock's subscription model which works out a lot cheaper.

Back cover copy – AKA the blurb

Once you have a front cover design you're happy with, the next stage in the publishing process is to write some descriptive copy for your book.

If you've decided to publish to Kindle only, you won't need the familiar back cover blurb that you see on books in bookstores. Your product description will be your blurb.

If you are publishing a print edition, however, then you will need some cover blurb, which should be regarded as a completely different beast to your online product description.

We often see writers using their back-cover blurb as their product description on Amazon, but this is a strategic error in our opinion. Your blurb might be catchy and cryptic, for instance, but this doesn't make for a good product description. The latter needs to be much more informative about what the product is and the benefits it gives to readers.

We address this important topic in great detail in Chapter Ten, because this will be one of your most important selling tools.

Back to the blurb…

Your blurb should be a short, catchy, exciting description of your book that captivates the reader in three or four paragraphs. (Whereas your product description should be designed to sell *all* the benefits of the book). Here are some tips for blurb writing.

Non-fiction

To write a non-fiction book blurb, scan over your chapter titles and focus on the ones that you believe deliver the main learning outcomes of the book. These are the things you'll want to mention in your blurb. A good non-fiction blurb should answer the same three questions we ask when considering a book proposal:

- Who is this book for?
- What's it about?

- What will the reader get out of it?

The potential reader will be looking at your blurb because the main title and front cover have enticed them to investigate further. The blurb now has to work to confirm that, yes, it is indeed the right book for them; it will meet their needs.

Don't be too wordy with your blurb. If you write too much the text will have to be smaller, making it harder to read, and in any case, you've got seconds to grab the reader and get your point across.

We advocate the "newspaper reporter" approach to writing your blurb. In the olden days, when newspapers were typeset by hand, reporters would put all the important stuff at the beginning of their article and write in short paragraphs. The less important, peripheral information was left until the end. This was so that, if the typesetter was struggling for space in the page layout, he could simply chop off any paragraphs near the end, because they weren't vitally important to the story. Layouts are done using software today, but the writing technique persists.

Think in terms of getting your most important points down first, and your less important (but still valuable) points to follow. Once you've written a rough blurb, edit it ruthlessly so that it flows well and doesn't waste words.

Here is the blurb Joseph wrote for his bestselling book, *Fingerstyle Blues Guitar*:

Fingerstyle Blues Guitar takes you from your first independence exercises right through to effortlessly combining chords, bass lines and melodies in the traditional Delta style.

The fundamental techniques of the acoustic blues style are taught in musical context through hundreds of usable licks. You will quickly build your soloing skills with syncopation, blues scales, vibrato, legato and other authentic techniques.

The first half of Fingerstyle Blues Guitar develops finger independence, 1/4 bass note lines, and musical feel through traditional vocabulary exercises.

The second half of the book applies these techniques to the essential chords and picking patterns of acoustic blues guitar and teaches you to combine chords, bass lines and melodies into complete musical pieces.

Fingerstyle Blues Guitar includes full solo studies and over 190 musical examples written in standard notation and tablature.

Download the free audio from **www.fundamental-changes.com**

Finger independence | Alternating bass lines | Chords and melodies | Syncopation | Picking patterns | Voicings and inversions | Authentic vocabulary | Complete studies and much more...

Now, you may not be a guitar player, but we're sure you can identify what's going on here:

- A one-sentence paragraph sums up the thrust of the book
- Paragraph two mentions one of the most important takeaways of the book: the person will learn hundreds of ideas and be taught specific skills
- Paragraph three doesn't impart much new information, but it elaborates on all the points mentioned at the beginning and also explains how the book is organised
- The next two paragraphs are short and sell important benefits
- The last paragraph highlights again everything the reader will learn. This text is bold to stand out and lazy people can jump right in here and see at a glance everything the book covers

We use this same approach to create the blurb across our entire range of books.

Fiction

Selling a novel through blurb requires a different approach. Fiction blurb is often character based – because vivid characters are the most important part of good fiction. It should also set the scene by introducing a conflict and setting out what's at stake. Here are a couple of great examples:

1. Killing Floor – Lee Child

Ex-military policeman Jack Reacher is a drifter. He's just passing through Margrave, Georgia, and in less than an hour, he's arrested for murder. Not much of a welcome. All Reacher knows is that he didn't kill anybody. At least not here. Not lately. But he doesn't stand a chance of convincing anyone. Not in Margrave, Georgia. Not a chance in hell.

It's a very short blurb, but gets right to the point. We learn the former career of the protagonist, something about his current life, and the fact that he gets charged with murder in some backwater where it's going to be hard for him to clear his name. All captured in just 61 words.

2. The Girl on the Train – Paula Hawkins

EVERY DAY THE SAME

Rachel takes the same commuter train every morning and night. Every day she rattles down the track, flashes past a stretch of cozy suburban homes, and stops at the signal that allows her to daily watch the same couple breakfasting on their deck. She's even started to feel like she knows them. Jess and Jason, she calls them. Their life – as she sees it – is perfect. Not unlike the life she recently lost.

UNTIL TODAY

And then she sees something shocking. It's only a minute until the train moves on, but it's enough. Now everything's changed. Unable to keep it to herself, Rachel goes to the police. But is she really as unreliable as they say? Soon she is deeply entangled not only in the investigation but in the lives of everyone involved. Has she done more harm than good?

This blurb is much wordier, but again we learn something about the main character: her daily routine; something of her state of mind; a hint about her past. We're also handed a mysterious plot: what exactly has gone on? What happened with the couple? How will it all be resolved?

One of the best things about this blurb is that it uses strong picture language. Whether you have seen the film of the book or not, you can picture the girl on the train and the couple on their deck.

Here are some of our top dos and don'ts for writing fiction blurb:

DO...

- Introduce important characters
- Set the scene for the challenge / dilemma / life-changing event
- Use picture language to conjure strong visual images
- Use words appropriate to the content. Don't make an erotic novel sound like *War and Peace* (or vice versa!)
- Learn the art of the blurb by reading the blurbs of lots of bestselling books

DON'T...

- Use clichéd language such as, "In this gripping, heart-stopping, blood-curdling..." etc, or "A roller-coaster / white-knuckle ride that will transport you to..."
- As with non-fiction, don't make your blurb too wordy or it won't stand out sufficiently and certainly won't all be read
- Get bogged down trying to describe too many details of the world you've created. Remember to show, not tell. Portray a sense of action and intrigue; don't waste words trying to explain your universe
- Give away the book's punchline (which should be obvious, but there, we've said it anyway)

We highly recommend reading *The Snowflake Method* by Randy Ingermanson. It's a fabulous book that teaches the fundamentals of book planning and how to write a gripping blurb.

Formatting your cover artwork

Now you should have your front cover design ready to go and your back cover copy written. If you are producing a print version of your book, the next step is to address the "flat" cover layout of your book. If you are only publishing via Kindle, you can skip this section.

"Flat" just means the artwork for your cover, flattened out, so that you can see the front cover, back cover and spine all at once. A high resolution PDF of your artwork, in this format, is what you will need to upload to KDP in order to publish the print edition.

The size of your front cover, without any bleed, is called the "trim size" of the book. You will have specified the trim size when formatting the interior of your book. Fundamental Changes books all use the 8.5" x 11" format, which is close to A4.

If you're publishing another type of non-fiction or fiction book, the most popular trim sizes tend to be 5.5" x 8.5" and 6" x 9". These are both standard US trade paperback sizes. The size of your book is important. Some authors have weird ideas about producing their book in a unique format, but if you want your book to be stocked by a bookstore, for instance, they have standard shelving sizes. Most paperbacks are 5.5" x 8.5" and 6" x 9" for a reason – they fit nicely on the shelves!

In order to create your flat cover artwork, you need to download a cover template of the appropriate size. During the setup of the print edition of your book (as explained in our downloadable guide: **http://geni.us/authordownloads**), you will have established how many pages your book runs to (e.g. 100 pages, 150 pages etc).

Armed with the details of your page count and trim size, you can download a PDF template that will show you exactly how the front, back and spine needs to be laid out for print. You can download KDP templates here:

https://kdp.amazon.com/en_US/cover-templates

Enter your details using the dialogue box on this web page and you'll have your template.

Choose your template

Trim size

6 x 9 in (15.24 x 22.86 cm) ⇕

Page count

160

Paper color

White ⇕

Download cover template

The resulting cover template will look like this:

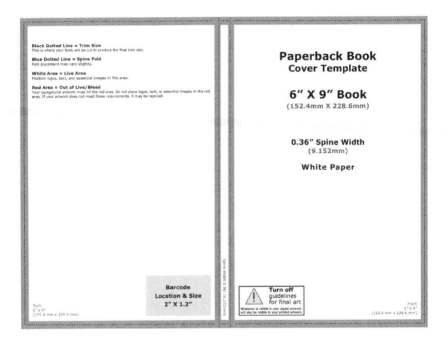

If you are using a designer, then you can simply pass on this PDF template to them and they will know what to do. If you are laying out your own cover using Photoshop or InDesign, we have video tutorials to guide you at **www.self-published.co.uk.** Here we show you how to add the back cover copy to your cover if you are designing it yourself.

Notice on the cover template that space has been left for the inclusion of the barcode. A book's barcode is generated from its ISBN. If you purchased your own ISBN, you will input this number when setting up the interior of your book on kdp.amazon.com and KDP will automatically place a barcode onto your cover art. If you decide to use a free KDP-allocated ISBN, you'll choose that option when setting up the book and it will be placed onto your cover in the same way.

When you're happy, you will need to output your artwork as a high resolution, print-ready PDF. (We explain this in our online guide, so don't worry about it too much now).

Chapter Nine: Publishing Your Book

We turn now to one of the most exciting parts of the process, because it's time to make your book live on Amazon. This is the final step of the *publishing* phase of the book, before we turn to the topics of marketing and promotion.

Once again, we've prepared comprehensive guides which you can download from **https://www.self-published.co.uk/resources-for-authors/** and will walk you through the process, but below we'll highlight a few important things you'll need to consider beforehand, and pay attention to when setting up your book.

1. Ducks in a row

It's worth mentioning here, in case it has slipped through the net, that by the time you're ready to publish you should already have a website that will deliver any bonus content to your readers. Don't hit publish until you have a basic website in place where you can host content.

Even if you don't have bonus content to give readers, ideally there will be somewhere people can go in order to find out more about you. These days there are lots of free tools with which you can create a simple, professional looking website without a degree in nuclear physics, so it's worth addressing.

Don't panic though, because we offer guidance on this in Chapter Eleven – Creating an Online Presence.

2. Automated checking process

KDP has checking processes in place for both print and Kindle editions. For the print version, KDP's automated process takes around 12 hours. If there are no problems with your book interior and cover art, your book will be live on Amazon between 24–48 hours after you began the publishing process. The Kindle process is slightly different. Once you have uploaded your file, the online checking process normally takes a few minutes, after which you can download a copy of the Kindle formatted file to check.

Allow enough time for the checking/publishing process, and don't get caught out announcing to your family and fan base that your book will be available on a specific date, only to discover it's not yet gone live.

3. Check the details

When you are filling in your title and subtitle, ensure they are written *exactly* as they appear on the front of your book. If you are adding your own ISBN, ensure it too is identical to the ISBN number recorded on the copyright page inside your book. These are little details, easily missed, that can cause frustration later if you get them wrong.

4. Error checking

Hopefully, if you've followed our publishing guide carefully, there will be no errors when you upload your files. The most common errors are:

- Cover artwork has been submitted without the required bleed (which can happen sometimes when exporting files from InDesign, or if the cover template was followed incorrectly)
- The book interior has page bleed when it doesn't need it (or vice versa). KDP checks to see if you have uploaded the right sized format for your book, according to the format size you chose earlier
- Low resolution images. It's very common to see a warning that images contained in the book are less than the required 300dpi. This can happen when a) you just didn't get the right resolution image to begin with, or b) if you imported an image and then stretched it to fit on a page. Resizing an image to make it bigger *decreases* the dots-per-inch resolution, while scaling an image down *increases* the resolution. The ideal is to work out what size image you need to begin with and import it in the exact size you need.

Tip: If you really need to use a particular image and simply cannot get hold of a 300dpi version, you can get away with printing black and white images at about 180dpi and they will look acceptable in print.

Anything less than 180dpi will begin to look grainy. Only do this in emergencies! Always aim to use 300dpi images.

5. Distribution

When you come to set up your book for publication, as you complete the section called "Rights and Pricing" there is an option to check/uncheck a box for "Expanded Distribution".

Through expanded distribution, Amazon can make your book available to online retailers, bookstores and distributors. Our advice is *do not* opt for extended distribution.

"But I want my book to be available in as many places as possible!" we hear you protest. Hear us out.

To make a profit, an online retailer must buy your book at a substantial discount. Whenever we have tested expanded distribution we've found that third party sellers were buying our books very cheaply, but then selling them cheaply on Amazon via vendor accounts, and undercutting us in the process. The results of this were twofold: first, we received a tiny royalty for those sales from Amazon due to the heavily discounted selling price and second, we actually began to lose sales because there were cheaper editions for sale alongside our own. For that reason, we never opt for expanded distribution.

To reach territories away from Amazon, the best thing to do is to sign up for Ingram Spark: **https://www.ingramspark.com** (a subsidiary of Ingram, the world's biggest book distributors), and use them to distribute everywhere *apart* from Amazon. There's a great article on Ingram Spark vs KDP here: **https://www.ingramspark.com/blog/ingramspark-vs-createspace.**

If you find yourself in the position where you've published a number of books and have a good track record of sales, it's possible to approach book trade distributors and negotiate a deal to supply bookstores and other online retailers. However, do this in your own right as a "publisher" (another good reason for having ISBNs for your titles).

If you feel you want to approach a distributor, here's another piece of advice: when we set up a UK distribution deal for our books we didn't offer them the entire list to begin with. Instead, we selected our 20 bestselling titles. First, because these had a great sales history and it was a no-brainer for the distributor to begin selling them, and second, because we wanted to partner with the distributor to continue to build our brand.

Publishing is an inherently risky business, because no one can really predict how a book will sell. Some sure fire "winners" have flopped, and some high-risk ventures have excelled against all expectations. In the publishing distribution chain, no one wants to be caught holding the baby, so distributors tend to be cautious about what they stock. Distributors never buy thousands of copies of your book (or even hundreds) – they buy small and often. Better to approach them with a solid proposition of books you know will sell.

6. Pricing and turnover

Pricing is an art. Do your research and understand what price books similar to yours are selling for. Understand though, that people with an established track record may be capable of commanding a higher price for their work than a first-time author. If you are publishing your first book, we suggest keeping the price towards the lower end of the scale. Initially your goal should be building a trusted brand and growing your audience and mailing list, rather than making money. If you do the first part right, the second part will follow. Become known as the brand who gives the most value and charges the fairest price.

At Fundamental Changes we publish non-fiction tuition books of around 106 pages. Generally, we will change $19.99 for the print edition and $5.99 for the Kindle edition. We have a few shorter books we've priced at $3.99 as tools for lead generation.

In other areas of non-fiction (such as business, self-help and spirituality), often the selling price is linked to the number of pages in the book. A 128-page book will sell for around £6.99 / $11.99; a 160-

page book is £7.99 / $13.99. A larger, 256-page book typically retails for £9.99 / $15.99 or higher depending on the content/genre. There exists a ceiling for this type of book, however, at around £12 / $18 no matter how many pages it has.

Fiction books are a different animal again. If the pricing was based on the page count alone, they would all be super-expensive, as many novels run to 400-500 pages. Publishers, and the book buying public, however, recognise the impulse-buy nature of fiction, so they are normally very keenly priced.

A paperback priced at $19.99 of circa 106 pages will generate a return of around $10 per copy sold. It doesn't take a mathematician to work out that if you sell several hundred books you will begin to make a decent amount of money. Because of the lower retail price – and because our books have lots of images, resulting in a larger download size and additional charges from Amazon – a $6.99 Kindle book will return around $3. If your book doesn't contain lots of images, your return should be greater. Alternatively, you could lower your selling price slightly to be more competitive.

Not including the books that Fundamental Changes publishes by other authors, Joseph's books (30+ full-length books, four compilations, three short lead generations books, and a number of foreign language translations) tend to earn between $1,000 and $2,000 per day.

7. Calculating your royalties

KDP provide a royalty calculator for the print edition of your book in Excel format. You can use this to experiment with your selling price, compared to the cost of printing your book, and see how this will affect your royalties. In the example below, we're testing the cost-to-sales-price margin on a standard 160-page paperback, printed in black and white inside. The average price for a 160-page non-fiction self-help type book tends to be $12.99.

kindle	direct publishing	royalty calculator		

Figures generated by this tool are for estimation purposes only. Your actual royalty will be calculated when you set up your book.

1. Enter interior type:	Black Ink
2. Enter number of pages:	160
3. Choose a distribution channel:	Amazon.com
4. Enter anticipated list price ($):	$12.99
Printing cost:	$2.77
Minimum list price:	$4.62
Amazon royalty:	$5.03
Expanded Distribution royalty:	$2.43

The calculator shows that you would earn $5.03 per book sold. We are very fortunate in Fundamental Changes that music tuition books justify a higher selling price. A one-hour guitar lesson with a reputable teacher will usually cost $30 per hour at minimum – and could be double that if they are a high profile player. Considered in that context, 100+ pages of good quality teaching is incredibly good value. This is what the typical Fundamental Changes book royalty looks like:

kindle	direct publishing	royalty calculator		

Figures generated by this tool are for estimation purposes only. Your actual royalty will be calculated when you set up your book.

1. Enter interior type:	Black Ink
2. Enter number of pages:	106
3. Choose a distribution channel:	Amazon.com
4. Enter anticipated list price ($):	$19.99
Printing cost:	$2.15
Minimum list price:	$3.59
Amazon royalty:	$9.85
Expanded Distribution royalty:	$5.85

8. Publishing for Kindle

You'll find our detailed guide on how to publish your Kindle book at **www.self-published.co.uk** but here we'll share a couple of thoughts.

i. DRM

Generally, we do not enable Digital Rights Management (DRM) on our books. This might sound like a mistake – surely we'd want to protect our assets? Our feeling is that DRM is relatively easy to get around for a determined pirate and is actually a nuisance for legitimate purchasers of the book who, understandably, want to be able to read it across their devices without jumping through hoops.

Some piracy is inevitable. Although it may seem a bitter pill to swallow, looked at positively, if someone reads your book and enjoys it, they may well go on to actually buy your other books. Plus, if they want your free bonus content, they'll have to join your mailing list! Don't worry about it too much – having people think your work is good enough to pirate is a high-quality problem to have.

ii. Error checking

Once you've uploaded your Kindle files, and Amazon's automated checking has done its work, you need to have a careful check over of the resulting file to make sure everything is OK. Kindle uses a file format called .mobi and it's possible to download the .mobi file for checking.

KDP has an online previewer, but we recommend downloading your file and sending it to your Kindle, or your iPad/tablet running the Kindle app. Sometimes the online previewer gives you the impression that everything looks great, but odd things can pop up in use, and the only way to know for sure is to read your book on an actual Kindle/Kindle app. This way you'll experience it as a reader and you'll soon see if any anomalies crop up.

Go through your book slowly and check any images are displaying properly. Check that breaks between chapters have been applied and ensure there are no new chapter headings in the middle of a page. Check your book in both portrait and landscape mode and turn off column viewing.

If anything doesn't look right to you, go back to the source file you uploaded and check that part. It could be a text formatting issue within Word, or an image that isn't quite sized correctly. If adjacent images seem to be "stuck together" you will need to add a return between them. If an image has been replaced by a red "X" then its dimensions exceed what a Kindle can handle.

Tip: *There is no point using an image bigger than 2560 pixels wide. The largest Kindle screen (Kindle Fire HDX) has a screen size of 1600 x 2560px and cannot display anything larger.*

If you're struggling with images for Kindle, there are some great resources on the web. Check out this article to help get you started: **https://www.thebookdesigner.com/2015/10/preparing-images-for-your-e-book/**

Be patient and work through the book slowly. It may take a few attempts to get the book displaying correctly and it can be a slightly frustrating process. Once you have worked through the Kindle book and corrected all the errors in your Word document, save the file and upload it to Kindle again.

Don't be tempted to short cut the checking process and say, "Well, it seems to be OK" because once your book is out, if there are anomalies it can lead to negative reviews, which you don't want. We guarantee that people will highlight any errors and moan about them!

Even after publishing many books, it still normally takes a couple of attempts for us to iron out any formatting errors. The most common error is forgetting to add a page break before a new chapter.

iii. Kindle pricing

Once you are happy with the look of your Kindle book, you can move on to the Kindle eBook Pricing page. If this is your first book, we would recommend a Kindle price of around $3.99. This is the average market price and, once you establish your reputation as an author, you can charge more. There is nothing to stop you putting in a higher price, but this is likely to result in fewer sales. Push for sales over profit to begin with – you are working to build your brand.

We also suggest enrolling your book in the Kindle Matchbook program. This allows customers to buy a cheaper digital version of your book when they buy a paperback edition.

Now you're ready to hit publish. Congratulations, your book should be live in around 12 hours.

NB: It usually takes a few days for Amazon to link your Kindle and paperback books. If this doesn't happen, email their support team via your Kindle account.

Chapter Ten: Writing an Excellent Product Description

Along with your front cover, your product description will make or break your book. You could have the best book in the world, but unless you let people know how it will change their life they have no reason to buy it.

We've talked about how to get a great cover design, and how to write a compelling blurb, so let's turn our attention now to how to write a great book description that converts browsers into customers. In a moment, we'll show you lots of examples and explain why we do things a certain way, but please remember two things above all. The most important principles we can teach you are:

1. Above all, sell the benefits

2. Think like the person who is searching

Both these principles need to work together in order to make a compelling sales proposition.

Don't just tell people what is inside your book, tell them what they will learn. Tell them how it will make their lives better. Give them the solutions to their problems. To illustrate what we mean, below is a case study of Joseph's book, *The First 100 Chords for Guitar*.

The book in question took about a week to write and was rushed out in time for Christmas 2016. It is designed to appeal to people getting their first guitar for Christmas. The book is priced inexpensively to encourage sales and get the reader onto our mailing list.

Content-wise, it is an incredibly comprehensive book that goes way beyond the bare minimum of information. It's 100 pages long and is the book we wished we'd both had when we were learning guitar.

Here is a simple list of what's covered in the book:

- Teaches the first 100 chords for guitar
- Basic chord progressions
- A little bit of chord theory
- Basic strumming patterns

- Contains diagrams and audio of each example
- Practice routines
- Contains some bonus content on building strumming patterns and chord sequences

This list is accurate, but it's not very inspiring. Below is our finished Amazon description in full. In a moment we'll break it down for you and explain our approach.

Master Essential Guitar Chords and Establish Good Habits for a Lifetime
- Discover how to play every essential chord on guitar
- Understand how chords work together
- Build chord progressions and master strumming
- Understand chord theory and construction
- Instantly apply and use chords to make songs

The First 100 Chords for Guitarists

Are you struggling to learn guitar chords?

Would you like an effective way to memorize, play and combine chords to make music on the guitar?

Do you want to confidently strum rhythms the right way?

Do you want to build perfect practice habits that will stay with you for a lifetime?

The First 100 Chords for Guitar will teach you to correctly fret, strum and combine the essential chords in music to become a better musician, quickly and easily.

Here's What You Get:
- A complete course, building from the first essential guitar chords to help you memorize, understand and apply chords musically.
- A proven practice routine that helps you build muscle memory, great technique and musical knowledge.
- Understanding of how to play chords the right way, and the theory of how they are constructed
- One instant trick to teach your fingers how to move - subconsciously

- *Bonus One: Learn to link chords together in a truly unique, musical way. Linking chords means practice is always fun as you explore creative ideas.*
- *Bonus Two: A complete guide to essential strumming patterns on guitar.*

Are you Missing Part of the Puzzle?

Most guitar beginners know a few chords, but few actually understand that it is quick and easy to expand that vocabulary into hundreds of chords and colours.

The First 100 Chords for Guitar is not simply a cold list of chords, it's a complete guitar method for beginners that teaches you how to practice for a lifetime of good guitar habits.

From the most basic chords, right through to some rich and exciting advanced voicings, you will be guided in small friendly steps. Throughout, there is an emphasis on using the correct fingers, changing chords smoothly, building great technique and developing creativity.

Test Yourself! At the end of each chapter, the newly introduced chords are combined into real-life chord progressions.

How to Practice! – Also included is a detailed 'How to Practice' section along with dedicated chapters on Essential Strumming Patterns and some Chord Theory.

Hear it!

Learning chords from paper is one thing, but once you hear how to apply them, they become music. The First 100 Chords for Guitarists contains many supporting audio examples to help you get inside the music, and quickly apply every new chord in a musical situation.

This book is Free on Kindle Unlimited

Now let's break this description down, section by section. Notice that everything we've written is true. Nothing is made up or exaggerated. The customer receives *exactly* what they expect when they purchase the book. Honesty is essential for your integrity. Don't lie to your customer.

1. The heading

"Master Essential Guitar Chords and Establish Good Habits for a Lifetime."

There is no need to repeat the title of the book in the product description, because the customer already knows what it is. Instead we create a newspaper style headline that is stating the book's benefits. It contains "essential chords" and will teach guitarists "good habits".

The reason for these choices is that students often fear they might be learning something incorrectly and be forced to undo bad habits later. Learning from a book is no different, so we wanted to reassure readers: this book teaches you the important stuff and the right way to do it, from day one.

2. The main selling points

It's OK to list your main selling points, but list them as benefits. Use active words such as *discover, understand, master* and *apply.*

- "Discover how to play every essential chord on guitar
- Understand how chords work together
- Build chord progressions and master strumming
- Understand chord theory and construction
- Instantly apply and use chords to make songs"

Using active words immediately makes the book personal to the reader. It helps them understand what they can achieve by having the book. In a sense, these words are "vague", because they will have different connotations for each person. The choice of words allows the reader to immediately imagine *they* are the person receiving the benefits of the book. The bullet points become about that person's journey, and are no longer an impassive list of facts.

3. Pain points

The next section takes a slightly different approach and sets up issues people are likely to be struggling with. It explains how the book can solve them. These are called "pain points".

"Are you struggling to learn guitar chords?

Would you like an effective way to memorize, play and combine chords to make music on the guitar?

Do you want to confidently strum rhythms the right way?

Do you want to build perfect practice habits that will stay with you for a lifetime?"

Pain points help the reader to further connect with the content of the book. Your goal is to craft pain points that make people say, "Yes! That's me!"

Well-targeted pain points are important because they confirm to potential buyers that the book is a good choice for their specific needs. At the risk of sounding facetious, if our pain points had been...

Do you struggle with bears?

Do you wonder how to keep pesky bears off your sandwiches?

Do your picnic baskets keep disappearing?

...the browsing customer seeking a good book on guitar chords would know immediately that the content was not for them!

Every skill we learn in life has pain points along the journey. If you're learning to fence with an epee blade for the first time, it's important to master the correct posture and stance if a) you don't want to get hit all the time and b) you want to hit other people all the time. Carefully thinking through the pain points associated with your topic will help you to write as though you have insight into the customer's mind.

Warning: You must ensure that the content of your book *actually does solve* the pain points, otherwise you are opening yourself up to a barrage of bad reviews.

Seth Godin says, "Marketers succeed when they tell us a story that fits our worldview, a story that we intuitively embrace ... but beware, if your stories are inauthentic, you cross the line from fib to fraud."

4. How the solution is achieved

Next, we let the reader know that we have the solution to the previous pain points and elaborate on how that solution is achieved:

"The First 100 Chords for Guitar will teach you to correctly fret, strum and combine the essential chords in music to become a better musician, quickly and easily.

Here's What You Get:

- A complete course, building from the first essential guitar chords to help you memorize, understand and apply chords musically.
- A proven practice routine that helps you build muscle memory, great technique and musical knowledge.
- Understanding of how to play chords the right way, and the theory of how they are constructed
- One instant trick to teach your fingers how to move – subconsciously
- *Bonus One: Learn to link chords together in a truly unique, musical way. Linking chords means practice is always fun as you explore creative ideas.*
- *Bonus Two: A complete guide to essential strumming patterns on guitar"*

By showing *how* this book provides solutions to the pain points we are further reinforcing the fact that this book is the real deal and will do what the customer wants. Again, these are benefits. The person is not just learning chords now – it's a complete course; it's a proven practice routine that builds technique and knowledge. Not only are they learning the best way to play chords, they are also learning music theory at the same time.

Notice the last two bullet points. As well as all the value described above, there is more. These describe content in the book that goes above and beyond its main purpose. These points are not directly about playing chords, but about useful, general musicianship that will further benefit the reader. They are a bonus in the sense that the customer might not have been expecting them in a book on guitar chords.

5. The round-up

Only now do we venture into anything like "traditional" book description territory. This section is a round-up of what has gone before, but we tend to put a fresh angle on the content, even here.

"Are you Missing Part of the Puzzle?

Most guitar beginners know a few chords, but few actually understand that it is quick and easy to expand that vocabulary into hundreds of chords and colours.

The First 100 Chords for Guitar is not simply a cold list of chords, it's a complete guitar method for beginners that teaches you how to practice for a lifetime of good guitar habits.

From the most basic chords, right through to some rich and exciting advanced voicings, you will be guided in small friendly steps. Throughout, there is an emphasis on using the correct fingers, changing chords smoothly, building great technique and developing creativity.

Test Yourself! At the end of each chapter, the newly introduced chords are combined into real-life chord progressions.

How to Practice! – Also included is a detailed 'How to Practice' section along with dedicated chapters on Essential Strumming Patterns and some Chord Theory.

Hear it!

Learning chords from paper is one thing, but once you hear how to apply them, they become music. The First 100 Chords for Guitarists contains many supporting audio examples to help you get inside the music, and quickly apply every new chord in a musical situation.

Download the audio for free from our dedicated website.

This book is Free on Kindle Unlimited."

This last section helps customers to identify again with any challenges they are facing. They will likely have searched for "guitar chords" or "learn guitar chords" or "learn guitar" on Amazon. We know what they are looking for, so we offer them tangible solutions. This last section is packed with yet more benefits, including the free bonus content (audio) that accompanies the book, which they can go and download.

We are still selling benefits:

- We're not giving the reader a list of chords – we're teaching them habits that will last a lifetime
- We're not teaching them isolated chords – we're getting creative and showing them how to create moods and "colours" with music
- The book is accessible and easy to use, with small, friendly steps
- It's a proven method – it will show you the correct fingerings, how to change chords smoothly, how to build great technique and develop creativity
- It has some academic rigour – "Test yourself".
- They can hear the music using the free audio, not just see it on paper
- If all of that is not enough, we let them know they can read this book for free on Kindle Unlimited

Meeting needs

The old expression goes, "See a need, fill a need." The trick is to help the reader associate their needs with the solutions you are offering and then sell the benefits.

It's not, "We have six flavours of ice cream."

It's, "We have six scintillating flavours of delicious ice cream, so you'll feel refreshed whatever the weather."

It's not, "Learn music theory."

It's, "Instinctively know how to play any song within thirty seconds of hearing it."

It's not, "200 examples and exercises."

It's, "Play solos like Eddie Van Halen and rhythm like Chuck Berry."

One last example. Stephen Covey was a management consultant, businessman, author and keynote speaker who wrote several ground-breaking books. One of his books was about time management and efficiency in business. *First Things First* teaches people how to tackle what's important, instead of merely urgent. Check out its product description below. It is incredibly economical with its words, but also incredibly incisive. It appeals to an issue most of us suffer with:

"I'm getting more done in less time, but where are the rich relationships, the inner peace, the balance, the confidence that I'm doing what matters most and doing it well?

Does this nagging question haunt you, even when you feel you are being your most efficient? If so, *First Things First* can help you understand why so often our first things aren't first. Rather than offering you another clock, *First Things First* provides you with a compass, because where you're headed is more important than how fast you're going."

Formatting your description

It's one thing to write a killer description for your book, but another entirely to get it to display correctly on your Amazon sales page. If you format your text nicely in Word, then cut and paste it into the dialogue box when setting up your book, once it's live you will discover that all you have is plain text; sometimes the paragraph breaks will have been ignored too. All that hard work for a block of plain text!

Fortunately, Amazon allows you to use basic HTML code, which can be used to specify heading styles, paragraph breaks, italics and bold type. The HTML is limited, however, so you can't add any images.

Unless you're writing a book on coding, you're probably not a dab hand at HTML and are going to need a workaround.

Dave Chesson has a free Amazon book description generator tool on his website: **https://kindlepreneur.com/amazon-book-description-generator/**

Alternatively, there are free text to HTML converters on the web. Try **https://wordtohtml.net/** for instance, which creates the HTML immediately as you type:

A fantastic resource we've often used is **http://www.betterbooktools. com**. They have a great Amazon description generator which also offers lots of advice on writing your description. They also have a fantastic tool that submits your book to many sites should you ever wish to offer a free promotion on Amazon.

Once you've added your description you can go ahead and publish your book. However, if you are serious about building your brand, you should first set up your website, create your social media presence, and set up your mailing list. We will turn to these topics in the second half of this book.

Part 2:
Websites, Marketing and Promotion

Chapter Eleven: Creating an Online Presence

Self-promotion

Someone asked us recently, "What is the difference between marketing and promotion?"

The traditional answer to this question is that marketing describes the totality of your commercial enterprise and is remembered by the 4 P's:

- Product
- Place (distribution)
- Price
- Promotion

Promotion is just one element of what is known as the "marketing mix".

A simpler answer is that that promotion is "telling people what you're offering" while marketing is "making them want to buy it". The management/marketing guru Peter Drucker said that the aim of marketing is to know and understand the customer so well that your product basically sells itself.

Tasks such as advertising, price pointing and time-limited offers come under the heading of promotion. Marketing is more fundamental – it involves creating a product that people want to buy, making it available where people can discover it, and selling it at the right price.

Good marketing and promotion are essential if you want to become a successful author. But you should know that if you want to be *really successful*, then you need to get your hands dirty. In promoting your book, you are essentially promoting yourself. Some people find that difficult.

Joseph has spoken at the Amazon Academy and the London Book Fair to groups of upcoming writers. After speaking about promotion, one lady was critical of the view that an author should be involved in marketing. She held an idealistic, purist view that a writer was someone whose sole purpose was to create art. Surely a writer shouldn't sully themselves by participating in the dirty act of selling their work? That would diminish the artist's integrity.

Joseph gently explained that art has never been like that. Michelangelo created art for patrons who gave him money and helped establish his status as an artist. This paid aspect of his career – creating art to order for a fee – freed him to create art without boundaries the rest of the time. Most of the greatest artists who have lived either sold their works to patrons or died poor.

Creative people love to create art, of course. Creative people who want to make a living from being creative, however, galvanise their efforts into something tangible and make small but necessary compromises. If you aspire to be an author and you currently see marketing as something you don't wish to do, we suggest you make that compromise very quickly.

A friend of ours played guitar in a great band. They gigged all over London regularly and were so good that their gigs were always sold out. One day they set up a meeting with a record company. The company loved them and loved their music, but they said they wouldn't sign them until they'd built up an online following of at least 10,000 people – and this was over a decade ago.

Being good at what you do is just one piece of the puzzle. The job of an author is not simply creating art. Even if you attract interest from one of the biggest international publishing houses, they will still expect you to have a large online following and an active mailing list. The book market is saturated and publishers know that books are hard to promote – so they look for potential authors who have already developed an audience – their own micro-market. Again, it's all about mitigating risk for the publisher. If *you* can build a following, then *they* can drive traffic, sales and make a profit.

We've said it before, but as a self-published author, you are both author *and* publisher. There's no middleman to take your profits and put limits on your creativity. If you can find your audience and drive traffic, you will sell books and dominate your niche.

For a long time, Fundamental Changes didn't do any advertising. We relied entirely on our mailing list, built from customers who had downloaded our bonus content. Since then we have learnt how best to use Amazon Marketing's Advertising Console (don't worry, we'll teach you how later) to promote our books, and we've used other tools to drive traffic to our website. Sales have grown tremendously.

Smart social media

If you want to position yourself for success as a self-published author, you cannot escape the need for online engagement. There are many ways to promote your book via traditional promotional methods – and we'll come to those – but *audience engagement is the new marketing*. If you're producing great books, then investing some time interacting with your audience will turn your customers into your brand champions. This is vital because we operate in what has been called the "recommendation economy" – a world in which 5-star reviews can boost sales without you having to do anything other than be consistently good at what you do.

Online brand and marketing guru Chris Brogan (check him out: **https://chrisbrogan.com/**) talks about employing the "B Strategy" and we think that, initially, it's very helpful to think in these broad terms. The B Strategy is:

- Be helpful
- Be human
- Be interesting
- Be everywhere

In short, helpful means helping prospective buyers with their questions – even before they've bought your book. Human means caring about your relationship with your audience. Interesting means giving your community something useful they can appreciate, rather than selling to them like a robot.

The last part – be everywhere – refers to the channels you choose to craft your online presence. Let's qualify that statement. Some people go nuts with social media and think they need to be everywhere. In fact, you only need to be *everywhere you need to be*. Everywhere that is relevant to you, the genre of your book, your topic.

For instance, if you're a fiction author, it might make most sense for you to have Facebook and Twitter accounts to post stuff of interest and interact with your audience.

If you're a non-fiction business writer, extracting short articles from your book and posting them to LinkedIn is likely to be a much better strategy. LinkedIn and Twitter may be your two best choices. Not so much Facebook.

If you're writing travel guides with photos, then Instagram and Pinterest could be your best bets. We were a bit late to the Instagram party, but we're making up for lost time now. Instagram is becoming huge for us so it's probably worth your time. Be interesting, take pictures, share it, add hashtags!

If you've written a book on strength and conditioning exercises for runners, you're likely to be posting interesting, engaging videos, demonstrating some of your content to YouTube, Facebook and Instagram.

The key is to consider, "Where will my audience be?" and make sure you are there too, posting useful content. Sometimes it's not easy to work out the answer to this question, but hopefully the examples above will help you to see where you *don't need to be*. If you're struggling to know whether you should use a particular social media channel, ask yourself this question: "Will my being here move a potential reader a step closer to buying my book?" If you can't say with any certainty that it will, you may be wasting your time.

Your aims for your social media presence should be to:

1. Increase people's awareness of your work. It's important that you set out to achieve this by posting genuinely (and we mean *genuinely*) useful content – not spamming the world with promotional messages and sales patter.

2. Learn about your customers. Engaging with a community of people who have an interest in what you do can yield all sorts of benefits. Sure, there will be the odd time-waster! But you can also discover what your community is crying out for and answer that need in your next book, and you may find that they have really good ideas that you can tap into.

3. Create a loyal fanbase – which you can do by being helpful, human and interesting and also by giving away free stuff that is of value.

4. Drive traffic to your website. For example, post a link to free content on your website and collect the person's email address when they download it.

In summary, you can't just throw random content into social media channels and see what sticks. Be purposeful and strategic about it.

A top tip is to check out **www.ifttt.com** (If This Then That). IFTTT is one of the coolest free apps around. It can connect anything to anything! If you have a smart watch and a smart washing machine, you could set it to turn on when your heart rate goes over 100 bpm, if you so desired! It can automate a wide range of tasks to help you work smarter. For instance you can post your photo to any social media account and see it everywhere. You can set it to share content from a relevant subreddit to your Facebook page automatically. You can use it to link your Twitter and Instagram accounts, etc. Employ this tool to connect all of your social media accounts and cut down on plate spinning. These days, Instagram can automatically post to Facebook, but it can be better to rewrite your post in a way more appropriate for the medium.

Your first website

Regardless of which social media channels you opt for, you're still going to need your own website. This is where you'll be able to present who you are and what you do in a way that suits you, without the constraints of the templated approach of Facebook and others. More importantly, your website will be the hub of your online presence. It's the place where you'll host any bonus content and build your mailing list. It's also the place from which you'll be able to drive traffic to your Amazon sales pages.

Everyone puts links to their social media profiles on their website, which is great for social engagement. But it sends people away from your site and, once on Facebook, they'll become distracted by other things. The ideal scenario is to send people to your website via social media and, once there, give them enough useful, relevant content to keep them engaged and motivate them to action.

When you became a writer, you probably weren't thinking that you'd need to become a website designer too! Don't panic. With the help of a well-established web platform (we are recommending WordPress), some free tools and plugins, you can create a simple, professional website to engage readers and collect signups – without a degree in computer science.

There are many things you could put on your website, but what are the essentials?

You can start with the bare minimum of around five pages, which should consist of:

- Home page
- About me
- Product page
- Content page
- Contact page
- Bonus content download page

Your home page should make it immediately clear what the site is about and have a clear and obvious navigation system that puts the site's different elements within easy reach. The home page could focus on you as the author, but should definitely feature your book cover.

A super-clean example of this is **https://www.davidsedarisbooks.com/** where the book is presented up front and the author bio is below. There is lots of white space and the menu system is clear and obvious.

A different take is **https://judymoody.com/** where the central focus is the character of the books, rather than the authors. But the animated navigation system is cool and, once again, it's really obvious where everything is.

Your "About Me" page should contain an interesting and concise bio. If you have an interesting story or reason why you began writing, then tell it. But keep it short and punchy. No one is going to wade through reams of text to get to the point. When you're J.K. Rowling, *then* you can write a long bio and everyone will read it.

Your "Product page" will feature your book cover and accompanying copy. On the Fundamental Changes website we use our Amazon sales description on our product pages, along with a clear link to each book's sales page on Amazon.

On your "Content" page, feature an extract from your book. If you're writing non-fiction this might be one principle you teach. Lay it out in a clear manner and back it up with any relevant bonus content, such as a supporting video, downloadable audio or a PDF. If you're writing fiction, you could include the full introduction/prologue from your book as a taster, to tempt people to buy the book.

Your "Contact" page should be simple and straightforward. Rather than putting your email address here (if you do, you'll get loads of spam), use a simple contact form plugin with a captcha mechanism, so that people can contact you via the form, and to ward off spam from web bots.

On your "Bonus content" page, this is where you add your MailChimp form and grab email addresses before allowing readers to access your supporting goodies.

Choosing a domain name

When you're ready to create your website you'll need somewhere to put it. There are numerous hosting providers out there. If you're using WordPress to build your site, then go for a host who specialises in hosting WordPress sites. We like,

> https://www.one.com/en/wordpress
> https://www.lcn.com/web-hosting/wordpress

Hosting generally costs a fixed monthly amount, or you can pay for a year up front to get a discount. A WordPress hosting package with everything you need will cost you about £60 / $80 per year. But that will also include extras such as support, an SSL (security) certificate, back-up and restore facility, and some sort of spam and virus protection.

Your provider will also be able to register a domain name for you. You can buy a cheap domain name from various providers, but the low-hassle option is to purchase one from the host you intend to use to save transferring it.

Choosing your domain name is a serious matter and one that needs thinking through. Joseph says that he made a mistake in setting up **www.fundamental-changes.com** because ideally it should have had the word "guitar" in it. Google likes it when the main topic of your site features in your domain name. However, now that we are publishing books for other instruments, it's less of an issue.

If you are creating a distinct brand for your books, then get a domain name that mentions your brand. If *you* are your brand, then go for your name. We recommend .com or .co.uk suffixes if possible. While you can choose many different suffixes these days, there is still some Internet snobbery around the perception that .com/.co.uk sites are more trusted and "professional".

We wished the job of choosing your domain name were easier, but it's amazing how many domain names are already taken. People have made millions out of domain "parking" (buying domain names they think will be popular and sitting on them, hoping to sell them for inflated prices in due course). It's entirely possible that your first-choice domain name will already have been taken, but keep trying until you find something that is short, memorable and contains your main keyword.

Via your hosting provider you'll have access to a control panel for your account where you can install WordPress onto your server space (fear not, they all have one-click installation processes) and create email addresses based on your domain.

Building your website

You can definitely outsource the task of creating your website to someone who does it for a living for less hassle, but this can get expensive. If you are reasonably tech savvy, you can build your own.

In terms of its simplicity, functionality and being free, WordPress is the easiest way to create a website in our opinion. There are other options, but we've found WordPress to have the best, most intuitive back end user interface, and there are many guides out there about how to use it. There are thousands of professional looking website templates for WordPress and over 75 million websites use WordPress as their platform.

We're not going to reinvent the wheel here and talk about every aspect of setting up a WordPress site. You will find links to the best online guides and articles on **www.self-published.co.uk**. Instead, here we will focus on the most important tweaks to make and plugins to use to get your site working for you.

1. Choosing a theme

If WordPress is the engine of your website, the theme is the chassis. The WordPress engine remains constant and you can "skin" your site with any design. There are thousands of free WordPress themes available on the web, and WordPress itself provides a good selection. Or you can buy a theme. **https://themeforest.net/category/wordpress** is a great source of quality themes at reasonable prices (typically $30). What's the difference? A paid theme is likely to have more features and come with some form of customer support, as well as documentation explaining how to set it up.

All of the themes on **themeforest.net** have online demos, which help you to see how they work and can be adapted to different applications. Generally, its makers will have thought of some common applications and created mock-ups. Search for "author" under the WordPress category of Theme Forest and you'll find some themes specially designed for those promoting books.

If you are new to this, pick a simple theme that is quite "clean" in its aesthetics and functionality. You don't need a host of special functions and it will cause less hassle in the long run. Remember, even if you are using a template, you can customise any aspect of your site. Nothing is set in stone.

However, do ensure that the theme you choose is mobile responsive and works well on a smartphone or tablet. If you like a particular theme, test it on your phone and iPad / tablet if you have one, and make sure it works well with no glitches or funny business!

2. Useful plugins

There are any number of custom accessories you can bolt onto your site, known as "plugins". A plugin will enhance your website or enable it to perform additional tasks, handling everything from search engine optimisation and Google analytics, to stopping spam comments.

The following are our recommended plugins. The majority are free, though there are some paid ones that are worthwhile having:

Akismet is generally installed by default when setting up WordPress. It helps to stave off spam comments on your articles

Amazon Link Engine. This automatically adds the correct geographical location for the user when they click on links to Amazon. In practice it means you can have one button on your website to send people to your book's sales page. Wherever they are in the world they'll get sent to their local Amazon store. This requires a small subscription charge and can be omitted if budget is a concern

MailChimp for Wordpress allows you to add a form that connects directly to your MailChimp mailing list. (If you're not using MailChimp then you should be able to find a similar plugin for your mailing list host. We presently use ActiveCampaign, but MailChimp is a great starting point)

Contact Form 7 adds a contact form to your website

Yoast SEO makes it easy to connect your site to your Google analytics and webmaster tools dashboards. Yoast also gives you guidance on how to make every page/post you create as search friendly as possible. When you add a post to your site, you should be creating searchable content for people interested in your niche. The important word here is "searchable" – content optimised to be found easily by the Google algorithms. Tell the Yoast plugin what word or phrase people will be typing into Google and it will give you a list of suggestions for your post that will make Google happy.

Insert Headers and Footers (very handy when you need to add a bit of custom code to your site's header or footer)

W3 Total Cache (makes your page faster so Google will like you more!)

3. Amazon Associates

Finally, sign up for an Amazon Associates account. This is an affiliate program whereby you can earn a small commission for directing people to Amazon via links on your website. If someone clicks through to your book from your website, you'll get a commission on that sale.

Not only does Amazon Associates give you a commission on every sale, it allows you to create unique tracking IDs which can be used to measure the success of any advertising campaign. Knowing where your sales are coming from is vital information for your marketing plan later on.

4. Having a blog

In WordPress, there are two main ways to present information: as a "page" or a "post". A page is a top-level, static piece of information that is equivalent to a chapter title in your book. Pages are for long-term, highly visible information that helps a user understand and navigate your site.

A *post* is used to display more in-depth content. A post is a quicker moving, more transient way of displaying information for a period of time, and it may be superseded in due course by other information.

The missing piece of the puzzle we've not yet discussed is whether or not you'll choose to have a blog (a way of organising all your posts) as part of your website. We recommend that you do if…

- You've got useful, worthwhile stuff to share
- You can use it as a way to add value to your readership

At Fundamental Changes, our blog is the heart of our website and what glues together our music-loving community. There you will find over 350 guitar lessons which are completely free to all. All the posts are categorised into styles, so if you're a rock fan, it's easy to find and browse all those lessons.

Used the right way, a blog can be a vital audience building tool. First of all, it's a great way to ensure you write on a regular basis. Second, your audience can get to know a bit more about you and your life. Third, people can randomly discover your blog posts when searching for other stuff, which may lead them to explore your writing further.

Many people think of blogging as dumbed down writing, but *Publishers Weekly* columnist and author Jane Friedman says, "If you approach blogging as something 'lesser than' your other published writing, you're more likely to fail at it… If you treat blogging seriously, all the writing or content that you generate for your blog can have another life, in another format or within another publication."

But what to blog about?

Friedman suggests that knowledge of one's audience and the questions they are likely to be asking is a good starting point for blogging. Talk about those questions and offer answers. If you're writing non-fiction, explain how your book answers those questions (in a non-salesy manner). Share your thoughts on themes and topics relevant to your audience. Failing that, blog about the craft of writing – the joys and challenges you've experienced.

The current model for website structure is to organise your whole site around a few pieces of *cornerstone content*. Cornerstone content could be a definitive post or page that contains excellent, definitive information, along with the most important revenue-producing links on your site (such as your product page on Amazon). Cornerstone content posts will contain the most valuable SEO keyword phrases on your site and you may only have a couple of them on your whole site.

Other site posts will link to this cornerstone content using supporting, but less important keywords. The idea is to create a "funnel" to the cornerstone page that sells your product. Most people won't land on your home page, they will discover a post by searching on Google. If this post, or sequence of posts, leads them naturally to your cornerstone, they will become invested and more likely to click your "buy now" link.

This type of structure is also (currently) what Google loves to see: great general content that leads to a few definitive articles. If you weave your buy links into this cornerstone content you should naturally begin converting organic browsers into customers. Think of it as a funnel where all the content on your site leads the user to a single outcome – the option to buy your book.

Best practice for website content organisation does change regularly, so the previous information is subject to change. One thing that is consistently true, however, is that genuine, informative content is the best way to get ranked highly on Google.

Use rich content like images and video. Remember that people often do image searches, so name your images with your search terms. Video is easy to create and helps users to stay engaged on your page, thereby reducing the *bounce* rate for your site.

Anything you can do to make your site "sticky" i.e. useful for your user, is beneficial.

Here are some excellent examples of author websites you could model yours on:

www.thecreativepenn.com
www.markjdawson.com
www.rachel-abbott.com
www.hughhowey.com

Chapter Twelve: Building a Mailing List

Building your mailing list

In the future, the most important weapon in your marketing arsenal is going to be your mailing list. But to build a mailing list you're going to have to gather emails from people who are interested in what you are offering.

Facebook

There are some great resources you can use to gather email subscribers by giving your work away for free (see "other ways to build your list" below). If you have a Facebook presence and want to use that platform to grow your fanbase, we recommend creating a community page for your writing. Notice we didn't say *author* page. You can get one of those later. For now, focus on building your brand. When you start to get bigger, or if you're writing fiction, you may wish to consider an author page to help people interact with you directly.

Setting up a Facebook page is simple. Go to **https://www.facebook.com/business/** and click on "Create a Page" in the top right corner.

Now choose "Community or Public Figure".

Now give your page a name and choose an appropriate category, as below.

Apart from adding graphics to make it look nice, that's basically it. All that remains is to fill in the information for the "about" section and you're good to go. If you've had a great logo designed and a nice cover for your book, use those graphics to make your page look professional.

The easiest way to get some followers for your page is to invite all your friends to like it, if you already have a personal Facebook account. You can also attract followers by sharing other people's content. Follow those whose content is relevant to your page. Also check out Reddit, which is a great way to find new things to share. Don't forget to *invite* anyone who likes your content to like your page. You can do this by clicking on the number of likes by each post and clicking "invite" next to each name.

Unique content is always better than sharing other people's stuff, but to create it is time consuming and distracts from the important business of writing your books. You can create your own content later, right now it's important to keep writing and building your brand.

So, once your page is up and running, how can you use Facebook to build your mailing list? Here are a few tips:

- Add a signup form to your page. MailChimp offer a widget to do this easily and will guide you through the process
- Facebook now has the facility to add a "call to action" button on your cover photo. This button can link to a page on, or outside of Facebook
- Run a competition to give away a prize in return for people signing up to your mailing list, such as a signed copy of your book
- Run a Facebook ad campaign to get more visitors to your page and more followers (we'll cover this in detail in the next chapter)
- Pin a lead magnet post to the top of your page. A lead magnet is an incentive for people to join your mailing list. Many people offer no incentive at all to sign up with dubious enticements such as "subscribe to our free newsletter". Yay! Instead, offer something tangible like a discount voucher for your books, free bonus content to download, or something else that is genuinely useful
- Add your books as products to your page

Organic reach

Over the last few years, we've grown the Fundamental Changes mailing list to over 60,000 people by offering free guitar lessons and giving away downloadable audio with our books. The purpose of the free lessons is simply to add value to our growing community of music fanatics, but a bi-product of this has been many potential customers discovering our website organically through Google searches (e.g. for "guitar lessons").

It's a great idea to add relevant content to your site. If you're working in non-fiction this could be lessons, articles, relevant resources etc. If you're in fiction, it could be book excerpts, character bios, quizzes, or articles covering your characters' back stories that don't appear in full in your books. Once people are on your website, if they like what you're offering, they can sign up to be kept up to date.

If your website is a reliable source of information about your chosen topic, then customers can find you in a multitude of different ways. Obviously there is Google search, but also through articles that have been shared to Reddit, Pinterest, Facebook, Twitter and LinkedIn etc. This can expand your reach significantly and traffic can begin to move both ways – from and to Amazon.

We're not big fans of popups that ask for an email address. They get ignored by most users and result in low quality leads to your mailing list. Instead of pop-ups, add a sign-up widget to your site that promotes an offer, such as a free book, article, or video, etc. Place it in a prominent location on your website.

Users who come to your site and find great articles and information about their interest for free will be willing to receive your offer if they think it will add to their knowledge. However, they will only be willing to part with their email if they feel that both your site, and your offer, are legitimate and genuinely useful.

You may be reeling at the thought of writing even more content after finishing your book, or may not like the idea of giving information away for free. However, you don't necessarily have to create any new content. You can share excerpts from your books, especially when you're first getting started. Content is king and repurposing your writing for a website post makes good sense. It's quick, effortless and you already know it is great content.

Giving work away for free is one thing that most people struggle with, but it is the cornerstone of every content-driven marketing strategy that has ever been successful. The benefits outweigh any potential concerns. We, and many others, have found that the more you give away for free, the more gets returned to you in life.

Look at it this way: people need to find your work to buy your book.

They will never find you if there is nothing to search for. You need content for your website, so it is a no-brainer to use a small selection of the work you have already created.

Don't give away the farm though! We extract two website lessons from every book we publish and often share videos of ourselves or other authors teaching the concepts. Not only does this create lots of original content for our website, it gives us multiple two-lesson series we can use in email automations that gets sent to our mailing list. A third email will promote a related book. These emails go out over time to those on our list who have shown interest in the subject matter.

We will cover the topic of email automation in Chapter Thirteen.

Tools such as OptimizePress can direct users to hidden content on your website once they have signed up to your mailing list. This means you can offer people exclusive "insider" content that you can host easily on your website, but which is not accessible to casual browsers. Notice that, so far, we've not tried to sell anyone a book – we've just given them stuff for free.

We also add a "tripwire". This is the offer of a half-price product, *after* they have received their free content. If the tripwire makes some money, we funnel that back into paid advertising, so that our ads are cost neutral.

Do NOT spam your growing email list. Add value with occasional content to your website that will interest them and occasionally send a newsletter. When it is time to launch your book, you can politely let them know it is available or offer them a pre-launch discount.

Other ways to build your list

If you're happy to give away a book for free or at a big discount there are a few resources that allow you to quickly reach thousands of readers and build your mailing list when they download your book.

1. Paid approach

www.bookbub.com is a paid promotion service that helps you get your discounted title in front of a huge, highly-targeted set of readers. With over 8 million members on their list, BookBub is one of the most popular mailing lists for readers. While paid promotions can be expensive, the results will normally cover your advertising costs and launch you high into the Amazon rankings. You will build your mailing list when readers start downloading your bonus content.

NB: You'll need to offer your book at a discount on every store it is offered, and you cannot use Bookbub if your book is in KDP select.

2. Free approach

www.instafreebie.com integrates with Mailchimp and allows you give away free copies of your book. It is reliant on you having your own social media, but you can also find Facebook groups dedicated to running joint author promotions. In a joint promotion, you link with other authors to share your social media sources and help to promote each other's work.

Be careful though. While it may seem perfect to get email signups from free offers, it's possible to create a mailing list full of people who only want freebies and won't ever spend a penny. It's better to add value and exclusivity to people who have bought your book using our bonus content techniques.

When I give away a free book, I normally offer a PDF version directly from my website. An alternative to this approach is **www. bookfunnel.com**. This allows readers to download your book in the most appropriate format for their device and it integrates with your mailing list to capture the emails of those people who download it.

If your book is enrolled in KDP Select you can make it free for up to five days in any 90-day period. There are plenty of websites that will promote your book while it is free.

If we run a free offer we use the form at **www.betterbooktools.com** to submit it to multiple sites at once. However, this is a paid subscription and if you wish to submit your books manually to promotion websites there is a big list here: **http://www.readersintheknow.com/list-of-book-promotion-sites**.

Chapter Thirteen: Email Automation

When you buy an item from an online store you are always required to give your email address at checkout. We're sure you know this isn't just so that they can send you your receipt.

When your email address is added to their mailing list it means the store knows you have bought from them before. They know that you trust them and are likely to buy from them again. If they're smart, they'll send you adverts that are related to the item you originally bought. For example, if you bought a cat bowl they'll hopefully send you information about cat food, not fish tanks.

In the above scenario, you are a *warm* audience. You've formed a relationship with the store and you're a trusted customer. If they send you useful content and interesting information you will start to build a relationship and will likely think of them when you're next shopping.

The absolute opposite of this is the scenario in which your email address is bought without your consent from a nasty company who sold your details. In this case you're a freezing cold lead. The company in question is unlikely to send you anything other than spam and you're almost certain to delete their emails as soon as they arrive. People who contact you in this way are normally trying to give your computer a virus or extract money from you illegally!

A different scenario is when you've willingly signed up somewhere to get some exclusive content. In this case you're a *semi-warm* lead. You may recognise the brand when they email you, but you've not bought anything from them, so don't have the trusted consumer relationship. You may still be reluctant to buy from them.

A name on your mailing list can be anything from completely useless to highly valuable. It is your job to develop a relationship with your subscribers and encourage them to trust you before they'll buy your products.

It should be obvious that warm leads are the best leads. If you can fill your mailing list with people who have bought from you before, you can form a great relationship with them and they will support you in your endeavours.

The most difficult task for an author is turning someone from a cold lead into a customer. To do this you must first *find them* (via adverts or organic reach), then *build trust,* before showing them products they might be interested in. If you can bridge the gap from "interested browser" to "customer", and ensure they are happy with your product, they won't hesitate to buy from you again.

There is a massive difference between someone who signed up to receive free content, and someone who bought your book and downloaded the bonus content. The first person is a prospect, but the second person has already trusted you enough to buy.

Moving your prospect from "interested browser" to "customer" is a big psychological barrier that needs to be broken. That's why making each of your books the best you can is so important – the customer will trust you because of the great experience you gave them. Each of your books is a permanent advert for your brand and if you can get people onto your mailing list as a result of buying your book then you'll have a high-quality list of customers who are likely to be repeat buyers.

The email marketing premise

The old-fashioned premise of traditional email marketing is very simple:

- Gain subscribers to your list
- Send adverts to subscribers

This is still the approach many email marketers take, but it's not the best way of doing things. The key to creating customers and fans is sending them emails they will *want* to open while keeping sales pitches to a minimum.

Build a relationship that engages your audience and don't spam them with adverts or unwanted content.

Until October 2016, Fundamental Changes had never spent a

penny to get someone onto our mailing list. Every person was added organically through downloading our bonus content. A list of over 18,000 people was built without really trying. In fact, while other people were paying big money to build email lists of lukewarm leads, we were literally getting paid by Amazon to add contacts to our list and build a great relationship with them. Here's how:

When customers buy our books, there is a very clear section telling them how to download the audio for their book for free. They enter their email and which book they bought, and are directed to the download page. Our signup form is connected to our ActiveCampaign account (**https://www.activecampaign.com/**). You can connect yours to MailChimp or any other provider.

The customer has bought a book, now they have their bonus content and they're happy. They've been added to our email list and now we can work to build our relationship with them and, hopefully, turn them into a fan. Remember, the best contacts you can have on your email list are those who have bought from you before.

List handling

Behind the scenes, a buyer's email address gets added to our mailing list. Our list is divided into segments, with a unique segment for every book we publish. This is a way to easily identify everyone who has bought the *Fingerstyle Blues* book, for instance. Our book topics are diverse, appealing to different genres of music, so segmenting is a way of preventing people from receiving emails about stuff they're not interested in – advertising a classical piano book to death metal guitar fans, for instance. Segmentation is a feature of all modern mailing list clients, so you can easily control who receives what.

Before discovering email automation, segmentation was as far as we went in organising our subscribers. Each week Joseph would write lessons for the website and send them to appropriate segments of the list. It was time-consuming but got great results. 80% of all the emails we sent only contained free guitar lessons, and were sent out every Sunday.

When releasing a new book, he would announce it to segments of the list for which it was appropriate and who might like to buy it. The resulting click-throughs to Amazon meant that the new book ranked highly on their site and started an algorithmic snowball rolling down a mountain. The book was promoted by Amazon to the relevant audiences, and because it provided Amazon with consistent sales, success became a self-fulfilling prophecy.

After a few weeks, everyone on our list who had downloaded the free audio for the new book was asked if they'd mind writing a quick review on Amazon, so that new customers who discovered it through Amazon's search engine would be more likely to buy it.

After the promotion period, we returned to sending out lessons until it was time to launch the next book.

The strategy of sending subscribers genuinely useful free content proved to be extremely successful, but Joseph found himself dreading Sundays. He had to write and record audio for a website post, write an email blast for his subscribers, then send it out. If there was a mistake, it got sent to 18,000 people! Then he discovered email automation and it changed his life.

Email automation

Email automation is exactly what it sounds like: a series of pre-prepared emails that are sent to specific groups at a set time and may be triggered by the actions of the subscriber.

The first automation was simple: when someone signed up to our list, they automatically got a welcome email to say thank you, along with a link to our other titles. If they had questions, they could reply to the email and our customer services assistant would help them out within 24 hours.

We realised that just because they'd bought *one* of our books, they didn't necessarily know about *all* of our books. This revelation meant that instead of promoting a new book only when it was released, we could promote older books, as if they were new, to a fresh audience.

We trawled through the email archives and dug out the lessons that had been the most popular. With these, a simple automation was built that sent new subscribers a mix of great lessons and sales emails each week.

Repeat purchases rose quickly for new subscribers and income skyrocketed, but Joseph still had to write new content each week for the older, more established users.

We started to understand the unlimited potential for email automation, but it was challenging to build the kind of automations we wanted, especially in MailChimp where (at the time at least) the complex if-this-then-else sequences were hard to program. It was suggested that we try ActiveCampaign and it was a big decision to move a large mailing list from one client to another, but it proved to be the right one.

Between us we decided that every new subscriber should first receive a short automated welcome sequence of emails once they'd downloaded their audio files. We would use this sequence to make friends and send them our best lesson content, so that they looked forward to our emails and would be more likely to open them.

This is our current welcome series:

- On day one they receive a video welcome from Joseph saying thank you for their purchase. We tell them that they're going to receive lots of free lessons and goodies over the coming days and weeks. We also ask them to add our email address to their safe-senders list.
- On days three and five they receive emails linking to the best free content on our website: video lessons, tutorials, useful content... you name it.
- On day eight they get an email asking them to review their book. Reviews make the biggest difference to a browsing customer's decision to buy a book on Amazon. You must politely ask your customers for reviews if you can.

When a new subscriber joins a list we add two "tags" to their email address. One tag tells us which *book* they bought, and the other tells us which *genre* that book belongs to.

We have five automation funnels – Blues, Rock, Beginners, Jazz and General Musicianship (books for theory and technique).

After the welcome series, subscribers tagged with "Blues" go into the blues funnel, the rock players go into the rock funnel, and so on.

Each funnel consists of a mixture of two-thirds free content and one-third promotional emails. We ensure that the content is extremely relevant to the subscriber's interests.

We use the book tag to stop the subscriber receiving adverts for books they have already bought. If they have downloaded a certain blues book, they will not receive adverts for that book when its turn comes to be promoted automatically.

Right now, if you were to download the audio for one of our blues guitar books, you would receive automated and personalised content for 40 weeks. It consists of multiple blues lessons from our website or relevant general musicianship lessons. Each content email is followed by an advert for a relevant book and this system works very well to engage and interest the list.

As you might have guessed, our mailing list also contains a large pool of users who have finished passing through the genre automations. We use a different approach to reach these subscribers. It's very simple: all we do is send out a single piece of content every Sunday to see who engages with it. This means that a blues subscriber may get a jazz guitar lesson, but if they click on a link we now know they're interested in jazz too, and we can possibly tempt them with some jazz books.

Consider this: we have thousands of different subscribers all at different stages in each automation. This means we are not simply promoting one book to thousands of people each week, we're promoting *all our books* to a few hundred people every week. In other words, if you're three weeks ahead of me in the automation you'll receive an advert for Blues Book 4 when I'm getting an advert for Blues Book 1. This produces a steady stream of sales across *all* titles, which Amazon's algorithms love (rather than one big spike, which is ignored in some of their ranking algorithms).

By feeding Amazon continual sales they continue to rank our books highly, so it is easier for potential shoppers to find them. Couple this with over 4000 5-star reviews and recognisable branding and you can understand how it's possible for us to dominate this publishing niche.

Email automation is one of the greatest tools we have. We use it to educate and engage our audience and drive a steady stream of sales to our books on Amazon. This, in turn, ensures the books continually rank at the top of their niches. At different periods, Fundamental Changes books have occupied all of the top spots in the music book category on Amazon – in itself, an incredible advert that has not gone unnoticed.

Your email automation doesn't need to be complex in order to be effective and it's easy to build productive automations quickly and efficiently.

As an aside, we often give away books at times like Black Friday and Christmas. When everyone else is sending out discounts and encouraging sales, we quietly thank our readers for their support and give them a book for free. We *hate* Black Friday with a passion, so it feels good to be able to go against the grain. All these little gestures add up, so when we do have a sale, people are even happier to buy our books.

A $4000 email

We can sell many of our books as PDFs direct from our website, because not all of them are exclusive to KDP Select. This means we can charge a little more for them and make more money per book than we do on Amazon. As good as Amazon are, not everyone wants to buy from them. One January, we ran a half-price sale for all PDF books and sent the following email to our subscribers:

FUNDAMENTAL **CHANGES**

Hi ,

Have a New Year's Resolution to play more guitar or bass in 2017?

Ready to pick up some sweet jazz licks or learn how to play the blues?

For New Year's Day I'm offering *50% off all PDFs at Fundamental-Changes.com*!

How do you take advantage of this deal?

1. Go here: http://www.fundamental-changes.com/book/

2. Peruse what's available on the site and choose your book (some books are exclusive to Amazon, but you can find most of the Fundamental Changes collection available here).

3. Click the "Buy PDF" button to add your chosen book to the cart.

4. In the Coupon Code space use "**NEWYEAR50**" and click "Update Coupon" to see your discount applied.

Want more than one book? No problem! Just return to this page http://www.fundamental-changes.com/book/ to add more books.

This is an unlimited offer, so you can buy as many PDFs as you like from the Fundamental Changes website.

But remember... **this deal only lasts until the 2nd of January 2017**.

Happy New Year from all of us at Fundamental Changes. Here's to a rockin' 2017!

Click Here To Get 50% Off PDFs

This email made over $2,000 in 24 hours, so we decided to extend the sale. Two days later we resent the email to anyone who hadn't opened, or clicked a link in it, with the subject heading, "Last Chance New Year Sale". In the next 24 hours we made another $2,000 – all from just one short email.

This campaign worked well because we don't spam our audience, and we very rarely do sales. There is no "secret marketing language" in the email. It just worked because we've spent time building trust with our audience.

Templates, branding and spam

You must consider how your emails are perceived by the recipient. It should go without saying that typos and broken links must be avoided at all cost, but there's more to it than just getting the content right.

166

All mailing list software allows you to use preformatted email templates into which you can import your branding and logo. You can select colours, fonts and signatures that remain constant throughout your campaigns. Companies like MailChimp give you hundreds of easily editable templates you can adapt, so it only takes minutes to create a style that represents your brand.

Avoid the excessive use of words like "free" and "giveaway". Only use these in context, as too many occurrences will get your email spammed immediately. In fact, getting out of Gmail's "promotions" folder is quite challenging these days and it seems that the only way is to ask your subscribers to add your email address to their safe-senders list immediately.

There are some free online tools that will protect your email from spam filters. Check out **www.mail-tester.com**. This service allows you to run your email through their system and receive a full report on how you can improve your writing.

An email will get better engagement if you include the recipient's name at the top. If you've collected this data on signup, you should be able to add a personalised "merge tag" that inserts it automatically.

Instead of saying "Hi" you can say, "Hi Bob."

There are hundreds of merge tags you can use to customise your content. This could be the name of the segment they are a part of in your list, or a Facebook like button, for example. Merge tags are an easy way to make it seem as if every email has been hand-crafted for the recipient and this massively increases engagement with your message.

The *subject line* is probably the most important part of your email. How it's perceived by the recipient will influence their decision to open it, or not. Avoid like the plague clichéd click-bait lines like, "You won't believe how much money this man saved with this one simple trick...". However, by adding a bit of intrigue you can raise the open rate of your emails quite successfully.

We recently used the subject line, "Discover how jazz chords *really* work", which got a huge amount of opens. Pique the interest of your reader in the subject, but make sure you deliver the goods in the body of the email.

Most templates allow you to add a short heading to the top of your email that appears in the inbox email preview. Use this to follow up and slightly expand on the subject line, to encourage the reader to open the email. We followed up the previous subject line with: "A handbook to the profound world of jazz harmony".

Avoid using too many images in your emails. It's normal to include a banner with your logo and a picture of your product, but go easy on images because spam filters don't like them too much.

Also, don't include too many links directly to Amazon. Multiple links to a commerce website can also easily trigger the filters. Use **Geni.us** links or similar to send the user directly to their correct geographical Amazon territory.

Above all, keep your message simple and clear:

- Are you offering them content?
- Are you promoting a book?
- Do you want them to fill in a survey to help guide your future releases?

You can use your email list for market research. When we've sent out surveys in the past, subscribers have often requested books on topics we've already covered, so we can simply connect them with the content and make some easy sales. Other times, people have suggested book ideas we'd never thought of, which sparked a time of writing new content and creating the products our fans are asking for.

A wonderful feature of hosts like MailChimp is that they will rank your subscribers by how engaged they are with your content. You can see who is opening emails and clicking links. Fiction writer Mark Dawson recommends making your most engaged subscribers into "super fans". You can ask them to be part of a "street team" – an early review and promotion group who get advance copies of your book, and who can spot typos and make suggestions about the content.

This street team can promote your book to their networks and will gladly write reviews on Amazon before you do a hard launch of your book to the rest of your list. Reviews sell books, so getting advance reviews will greatly increase your long-term sales.

A carefully curated email list can help you to do market research, get reviews, build relationships, promote your books and even raise money for good causes. Nurture it, use it wisely and treat your subscribers like friends, as they will dictate the long-term success of your business.

A/B testing and other tools

All mailing list providers give you useful tools to boost engagement and gain clicks. One of the best tools allows for "A/B testing". In other words, you can try out different versions of your email and then automatically send the one that is getting the most engagement.

The most obvious variable to test is your subject line, because it is the most important factor in dictating whether your email gets opened. You can try out subtly different subject lines or ones that are wildly different.

The system initially sends both emails to a small section of your list, say 20% (half get subject line A and half get subject line B), and monitors the emails for engagement. After about four hours, it will automatically send the winning email to the other 80% of your list.

Most hosts offer a quick button to resend your email to people who didn't open it the first time. You could also alter the subject line to see if you can get more engagement. Don't do this more than once though, as you'll start to annoy people and get spammed. We often find that we can get 5-10% more opens on an email by using the "resend to unopens" function.

It is important to keep a "clean" list, so if you notice that a growing number of people aren't opening your emails, try sending them a three-part re-engagement campaign. Offer them an amazing promotion on a book – maybe 70% off. If they don't engage, resend the offer a few days later with a new subject line. Finally, send them a "last chance" email. If this doesn't get any engagement, then it is time to delete them from your list.

Keeping a clean list is important because spam filters will penalise you if you continually get a high percentage of unopened emails. It's better to focus on the people who want to hear your message and say goodbye to the people who never open your emails. It's a tough call, but it's the right decision.

Launching a book to your mailing list

We used to think that we were doing a good job if we launched a book to our mailing list and got an initial spike of sales. It was really gratifying to see all those downloads and paperback purchases making a big pointy line on the graph. The ranking algorithms certainly picked up on this and our guitar books could sometimes be found in the top 1000 books on *all* of Amazon, which only took about 300 sales per day.

We would then begin to receive reviews and leave the book alone to gather momentum. The books always continued to sell because they're part of a trusted brand, are well reviewed, and represent great value. Also, music tuition books have a very long "tail" (there are always new musicians), so even the very first books we published continue to sell very consistently.

Recently, however, we've found that this single launch approach isn't the best way to launch a new book. One of Amazon's main ranking algorithms seems to totally ignore sudden spikes of sales, so it is better to launch your book to your email list gradually, rather than all at once.

A large portion of our email list is interested in blues guitar (about 20,000 people), so if we launch a new blues book, we'll do it slowly, sending to around 5,000 people at a time with a couple of days gap in between. This avoids the initial spike and spreads launch sales over a period of weeks, while still getting the book to #1 on the Amazon guitar book charts.

We back up the mailing list launch with social media posts to try to ride the wave as long as possible, as well as launching several Amazon Advertising Console ad campaigns – the topic to which we'll turn next.

By spacing out our sales over a longer period, the Amazon algorithm that looks at monthly (instead of hourly) sales is much happier and more people get to see the book. Usually, due to the distinct branding and the number of other titles we've published, sales of other titles will lift during this time. It's a much better system than having one big launch and sets a book up for a long and successful future.

Chapter Fourteen: Amazon Marketing Services

Amazon Marketing's Advertising Console is Amazon's own pay-per-click advertising platform. Initially, only books enrolled in the KDP Select program had access to the program, but in 2016 this changed and Advertising Console was opened to all authors selling books via KDP.

The introduction of Advertising Console was a game-changer for independent authors and the results can be astonishing. Facebook adverts can be useful to drive traffic to your books from outside the Amazon environment, but Advertising Console enables you to put your book directly in front of people who are actively looking to buy it. People browsing Facebook aren't normally in a buying frame of mind, they're there for the cat videos, but if someone is browsing Amazon it's hard to think of a reason they'd be there without the intent of buying something.

Advertising Console allows you to target potential customers with pinpoint accuracy. Your adverts are triggered by a selection of keywords – i.e. what people might be searching for. If you've been careful to craft your book title, subtitle and product description with relevant, keyword-rich content, Advertising Console works beautifully. You pay for each click through to your book's sales page, but the clicks can be very cheap and the conversion rate is very good.

Some fiction authors complain about struggling to make Advertising Console work for them, and here non-fiction writers do have a clear advantage. The descriptions of non-fiction books are often filled with terms people might be searching for. But if you fancied discovering a great novel by an author you'd not read before, how would you go about it on Amazon? You might reasonably type in, "new fiction books" or "new releases fiction". That's going to result in a plethora of options and you're still a needle in a haystack. People searching for a book on playing blues guitar, however, will probably type in "play blues guitar" or "blues guitar book" – all strong keywords we will have used in our description.

As well as appearing in search results, Advertising Console places adverts on the product pages of *related* books. So even if the customer doesn't click on one of our books in the search results, it's likely they'll see one anyway, with its 5-star reviews and killer description. Plus, we run adverts for all of our books continually, which means there are 100+ books being promoted, and our branding appears on almost every guitar book product page.

Amazon also promotes our titles via its "customers who bought this book also bought" adverts. Here are two screenshots from Amazon. The first is of one of our blues guitar books and the second is a competing blues guitar book. Notice the bottom half of the screen where you can see our other books.

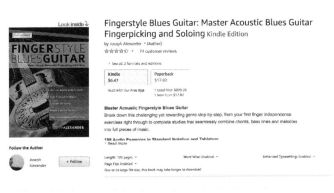

Customers who viewed this item also viewed

Sponsored products related to this item (What's this?)

Although you are probably setting out to write a different kind of book, it's hard for us not to encourage you to write a series of detailed non-fiction guides about your chosen subject. The way to make millions on Amazon is to write multiple books, develop a strong brand identity, and get a steady stream of sales via email automation.

Before advertising your book on Advertising Console try to get some reviews. Reviews are perhaps the biggest factor in a customer's decision to buy a book. You don't need many, but seeing five stars next to your book will help to drive sales. Remember to ask people who have signed up to your mailing list to review your books and your sales should start to rise exponentially.

Creating an Advertising Console advert

If you're a non-fiction author then setting up an Advertising Console advert takes about 60 seconds and Amazon will do most of the work for you. If you're a fiction writer it can be more challenging, as you'll have to think carefully about manual keyword targeting.

To get started, log into your Amazon KDP account and click on "promote and advertise" next to one of your books.

The paperback version has its own Promote and Advertise button:

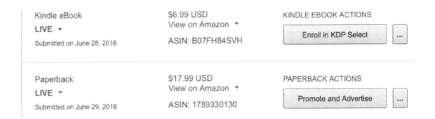

To promote the Kindle edition, click on the small button with three dots and select "Promote and Advertise" from the floating menu:

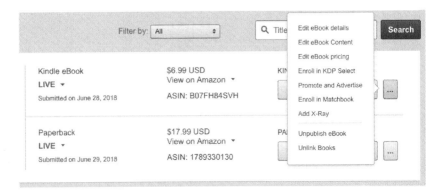

This will take you to the following web page. Click on "Create an ad campaign".

Promote your book on Amazon

Run an Ad Campaign

Promote your book through advertising on Amazon.com. At this time, Amazon Marketing Services is only available in English. Learn more

Create an ad campaign

You will have to go through the approval process if this is your first time, but once you're set up, in future you can navigate straight to **https://advertising.amazon.com/** and sign in with your normal details.

- Create a Sponsored Product advert (we've had no success with Product Display Ads)
- Select the book you wish to advertise from the drop-down menu
- Give the campaign a clear, memorable name matching the title of your book
- Set the budget to $5 a day
- Run the campaign continuously and don't forget to monitor it! Advertising Console seems to update about every three days, so it may take a little while before you see your results
- Select Automatic Targeting
- Set the CPC (cost per click) to $0.30
- Paste a juicy part of your product description into the Customise Your Ad field. Ensure you use important keywords for your book to please Amazon's algorithm. There is a limit of 150 characters
- Submit your campaign for review
- You're done!

This may seem a bit too easy, but it is the most successful Advertising Console strategy we've used as a non-fiction publisher. We believe it works so well because our titles, descriptions and content match closely to the content of the Customise Your Ad field. This is another reason why we set the targeting to Auto – Amazon knows better than us what people are searching for and they generate the keywords based on the title and description of the book.

We have experimented with manual targeting with mixed success – some adverts do very well, but some simply don't work at all. But if you've written your title, subtitle and product description well, and you've used closely related keywords in the Customise Your Ad field with some tantalising text, you shouldn't go far wrong. Manual targeting seems to be much more appropriate for fiction writers, where customers are not searching for terms that are specific to the subject of the book. The diagram below shows a snapshot of the results we've been getting using Advertising Console with auto-targeting:

Sponsored Products	11/13/2016	–	Daily: $10	165,744	760	$0.13	$99.68	$1,190.76	8.37%	Copy
Sponsored Products	11/13/2016	–	Daily: $5	151,229	578	$0.14	$81.17	$703.23	11.54%	Copy
Sponsored Products	11/13/2016	–	Daily: $3	132,714	402	$0.13	$52.87	$625.74	8.45%	Copy
Sponsored Products	11/27/2016	–	Daily: $5	1,099,108	1,237	$0.16	$198.15	$1,400.05	14.15%	Copy
Sponsored Products	11/27/2016	–	Daily: $5	341,093	379	$0.11	$59.84	$440.60	9.04%	Copy
Sponsored Products	11/27/2016	–	Daily: $6	260,814	250	$0.14	$34.96	$193.97	18.02%	Copy
Sponsored Products	11/30/2016	–	Daily: $5	694,244	999	$0.17	$165.32	$1,104.07	14.97%	Copy
Sponsored Products	11/30/2016	–	Daily: $5	440,042	622	$0.17	$103.35	$704.32	14.67%	Copy
Sponsored Products	11/30/2016	–	Daily: $5	146,505	177	$0.13	$22.29	$138.76	16.06%	Copy
Sponsored Products	02/15/2017	–	Daily: $5	1,353,753	1,361	$0.15	$206.48	$1,505.30	13.72%	Copy
Sponsored Products	02/22/2017	–	Daily: $5	841,147	1,012	$0.15	$153.35	$1,227.98	12.49%	Copy
Sponsored Products	04/03/2017	–	Daily: $5	25,343	155	$0.15	$23.47	$204.48	11.48%	Copy
Sponsored Products	04/03/2017	–	Daily: $10	59,783	341	$0.14	$48.23	$394.55	12.22%	Copy
Sponsored Products	04/03/2017	–	Daily: $5	51,010	220	$0.15	$32.28	$284.50	11.35%	Copy
Sponsored Products	04/03/2017	–	Daily: $4	45,353	31	$0.18	$5.72	$35.76	16.00%	Copy
Sponsored Products	04/03/2017	–	Daily: $5	423,495	622	$0.18	$112.94	$787.25	14.35%	Copy
Sponsored Products	04/03/2017	–	Daily: $5	74,510	62	$0.17	$10.49	$71.87	14.60%	Copy
Sponsored Products	04/03/2017	–	Daily: $5	929,513	1,075	$0.15	$162.21	$1,156.95	14.02%	Copy
Sponsored Products	04/03/2017	–	Daily: $5	590,399	787	$0.14	$113.87	$911.67	12.49%	Copy

All these adverts combined took about 60 minutes to create. Looking at the top advert in terms of revenue, you can see that we spent $156 to return $1283. The final column in the screenshot gives a percentage figure for average cost of sale (ACoS). Ideally, we would like this figure to be below 15%. Some are lower, but our absolute max is 20%. If the average cost goes over 20%, we conclude that the ad is not working as it should and we simply kill it off.

Note that this revenue is the total sales of these Kindle books, but does not account for Amazon's 30% cut. Even so, it represents a huge return on investment.

We must stress that there is no magic formula for Advertising Console ads, we just set and forget! If an advert is working well, we increase the budget per day. In a niche genre such as ours it is difficult to max out a $5 per day budget when the CPC is just $0.15.

Here is the exact text for our most profitable advert:

Sponsored ⓘ

Guitar: The First 100 Chords for Guitar: How to Learn and Play ... Nov 17, 2016
by Joseph Alexander

Proven practice routines that build from the first essential guitar chords to help you memorize, understand and apply chords musically in songs.

★★★★☆ 70

If auto targeting isn't working for you, Advertising Console will generate a list of likely search terms from your book title. You can also check out Google's keyword generator for inspiration and look at other books in your niche that are selling well. Use your gut feeling to put together a list of keywords for your advert and monitor the results closely.

If a keyword seems obvious and is getting clicks but no conversions, it is likely that the problem is with your book cover or product page. Do you have good reviews to convince readers that your book is a great product? Trusted and verified reviews are so critical to your marketing strategy, as trusting the herd is a deep part of the human psyche.

But Amazon Advertising Console is definitely worth a great deal of consideration and can easily be worked into a marketing plan for your books.

Chapter Fifteen: Freelancers and Translators

In traditional publishing, it has always been the norm for publishers to employ all the skills they need in house. Editors, designers, rights sales personnel, copywriters, you name it. But today the freelance market is huge. The growth of the gig economy means that many talented people are working for themselves from home, to have a life-work balance that suits them. This means that all the skills you need to complete the publishing process are out there somewhere – it's just a case of finding the right people who suit your budget, workflow and needs.

Joseph writes,

When I first started writing I did everything myself. I discovered the long, time-consuming ways of doing everything and then worked hard to increase my efficiency. I have my father to thank for this. He would pay me to do small jobs like stuffing envelopes when I was young, watch me for a while, then suggest improvements to my workflow, so I could be more effective and earn more allowance!

I applied this concept to my writing and made sure I never had to do a job twice if I didn't need to. I started with my book layout template in Word and added keyboard shortcuts and macros. When I made a diagram in Photoshop, it was logically filed, so I never had to make it again and could find it quickly. By using a Photoshop template, I developed front cover branding and could create a good-looking cover in a matter of hours rather than days.

I invested in software to quickly create music notation and chord diagrams that saved me hundreds of work hours and, again, created keyboard shortcuts to save me thousands of clicks.

I realised I could ask someone to start checking my book when I was only halfway through writing it. I'd be finished before they were, so I could commit their changes to my manuscript and design my cover while they worked through the second half of the book.

It was more beneficial to pay someone to record my audio examples when the book was only half finished, instead of waiting until the book was done and recording them myself. The extra few days of sales more than made up for the cost of recording and I could focus on getting my launch right.

All these little efficiencies added up, but there were still too many things to think about when running my business.

* * *

Growth is a challenge to any business and success brings its own problems. For the individual author, the most obvious challenge is spreading yourself too thinly. As your publishing expands, so do the jobs that need doing and, if you're not careful, these can drag you away from the important task of writing more books. You can find yourself turning into an administrator. Among the things you'll find yourself doing are:

- Writing website content
- Answering customer emails
- Interacting with any other authors you decide to publish under your brand
- Paying suppliers
- Giving customers technical support
- Accounting/running a Limited company
- Managing Amazon (adding products and running Advertising Console campaigns)
- Writing and sending mailshots
- Running social media
- Dealing with the tax man!

The list goes on, but it is inevitable that the more books you publish, the more admin you'll do and the less time you'll spend simply writing. Both of us, at different times and in different ways, have found ourselves working way too hard and putting in too many hours. Eventually we both realised, independently, that it was stressful and unhealthy. Something needed to be done.

One of the biggest time-sucks was responding to technical emails. You would not believe the number of people who can't follow the simple instructions to download an audio file! A typical email went something like,

"The audio for your book doesn't work. Please help as I don't want to have to leave a bad review."

Full marks for brevity, but the customer doesn't tell us which book they've bought or what platform they are using. So ensued a long, drawn-out exchange of emails consisting mainly of fact-finding on our part. Which book did they buy? What device are they trying to download it to? What operating system are they on? What were they trying to do that wasn't working?

As you can guess, this was a time-consuming and fatiguing process. After a few dozen of these, one is not in a creative mood to sit down and write fresh, inspiring content. Helping customers is important, but we had to be free to do what was *most* important – creating new books.

The solution was hiring Aya – a lovely lady who works from home in the Philippines to take care of all the technical support emails. She receives all the emails that come through the contact form on our website. We wrote some templated responses for her, since most people had the same problem and we were asked the same questions time and again. Aya has been working with us for four years now and also helps us with social media and preparing the royalty reports to pay our authors.

We discovered that the average wage in the Philippines was around $250 a month for about 230 hours of work. Aya works 30 hours a month for us and earns $150. We're both very happy with the arrangement. She is extremely committed to her work, produces excellent results, and consistently performs better than anyone we've worked with in the UK! She saves us hundreds of hours of time and frustration each month, because she can achieve in one hour what we achieve in four. We don't have to deal with any technical enquiries and she forwards any emails that require a personal response.

We found Aya through **www.upwork.com**. Anytime we need to outsource work we simply post a job advert with our requirements and wait for the responses to roll in. Then we narrow down the field to the best responses and send some further questions to the best candidates. Once we are down to the best three candidates, we conduct Skype interviews and select the best applicant for the job. Through Upwork we've used the services of,

- Virtual Assistants
- Graphic Designers
- Cover Artists
- Translators
- Transcribers
- Compositional Arrangers
- Writers
- Web Designers
- WordPress Data Entry
- Facebook Marketers
- ActiveCampaign/MailChimp experts
- Copywriters
- Copyeditors
- Proof Readers
- Video Editors
- Guitarists to record audio examples
- Bass players to translate guitar books into bass books

The list goes on...

We don't use freelancers for everything. Between us we handle the tasks of writing, editing, InDesign layouts, cover design, new author acquisitions and Advertising Console campaign management. We are fortunate in that we have very complementary skill sets and have established a very efficient workflow.

You may currently be at the stage where you are having to do absolutely everything yourself and look forward to the time when you're earning enough from book sales to outsource some of those tasks. Well, it took us quite a while to reach that point and build up sufficient income to employ others. A big disadvantage of the old fashioned model of employing everyone you need is that publishing programs ebb and flow. Sometimes you are manically busy and other times you're not. It's painful to see people you are paying sitting around twiddling their thumbs when it's not so busy! This is why outsourcing to freelancers is so effective and cost-efficient. You only pay for what you need when you need it.

Also, it has to be said that no one can be exceptional at everything, no matter how gifted they are. You could spend hours toiling over a social media post design only for it to look mediocre when you're done. Or, you could ping it over to a designer who eats this stuff for breakfast and they'll have it done in no time and it'll look 100 times better.

In Fundamental Changes, transcribing music can be a time-consuming, exhausting task either of us would lose hours on. Or, we could just pay our author Levi Clay to do it, who is a transcribing ninja and the most in-demand transcriber in the UK.

You get the idea.

We've also sought to connect our freelancers together for certain tasks and instructed them to work within a set budget. The person running our social media campaigns can ask our designer for graphics when needed without asking our permission. When an author has output the notation for their book as high resolution PDFs, they can send it to Irene, the lady whose job it is to crop and flatten those images, and cut them into separate sections, so that they can be inserted into the final text of the book.

Here's a magic tip: *You can easily set up an IFTTT recipe that will send a notice via Gmail when a file is added to a specified Dropbox folder, so freelancers can be alerted without your intervention.*

As your book writing business grows, invest in freelancers to save your time and sanity. If there is any task you find yourself repeatedly performing and not enjoying, invest a small amount of money to get it taken care of.

Writing the perfect job description

When you post a job on Upwork you'll get hundreds of people replying, many of whom will copy and paste their resume without reading your job description.

To quickly find out who isn't paying attention, ask all applicants to reply with a specific phrase. We always ask applicants to reply with the phrase "I am a human", because we suspect there are a few auto-response bots being used!

It doesn't matter how good the rest of their application is, if they don't have "I am a human" in the first line of their reply, it gets deleted. In fact, we don't even read the submission. If someone is going to apply for a job without reading the description carefully, there is no way we can trust them with our brand.

Next, we place a random question in the middle of the post, such as, "What is your favourite animal?" If this question isn't answered, we'll most likely ignore the applicant.

The main body of your job post should go into detail about what you need and expect from the right person. Ask pertinent questions about how the applicant sees their role and what results they think they can achieve. Ask what you can provide them with so they can do their best work. Never give out your website in the initial job posting. We were looking for a WordPress expert once and made this mistake. We got spammed by marketing companies for weeks.

There's not much more to it than that. Whittle down the pack and interview the strongest contenders via Skype. Always go with your gut feeling when hiring. You'll be developing a working relationship, so it's vital to communicate well and have a good rapport.

Two things you should bear in mind:

1. Hire slowly and fire quickly

Be slow to make the decision of hiring someone, especially if they'll have access to your Facebook account, mailing list or credit cards. If you find that their work is below par, get rid of them quickly. That might sound harsh, but there are plenty of great freelancers out there.

We rarely have problems with freelancers, and some are now good friends, but you'll save a lot of hassle if you take a hard-line view on failure.

2. You're dealing with real people

Pay your freelancers well and treat them right. They're not robots; they have families and needs. We have worked with a lot of people in the Philippines, which is still a developing country in many ways. When one lady asked us for $1.50 an hour during her trial, we refused and insisted on paying her $4 immediately. While this isn't a massive sum by western standards, paying her 150% more than she'd asked for enabled us to sleep well at night, knowing that she could have a decent standard of living. Since then, she has had two pay rises and is one of our most trusted employees.

Typhoons hit the Philippines in certain months, so you must be understanding if a worker is unavailable during that time. Power lines go down and areas get flooded. If you're not OK with this then you're going to have a tough time, but Romania is another great source of talent.

While we've had great experiences with freelancers from many countries, the most loyal, friendly and hardworking people always seem to come from the Philippines. We'll often filter searches to just that country when we're looking to invite a freelancer to apply for a job. Due to the differences in our economies you can pay a great wage to someone in the Philippines and get skills comparable to, or much better than, back home.

Someone once accused Joseph of being a traitor to his country by not employing people in the UK. He thought about it for a minute, then asked the person, "So you're saying a human life in the UK is worth more than a human life in the Far East?" When they had no response, he told them exactly how much tax Fundamental Changes pays the UK government each year. It was more than his annual salary.

Translations

When Amazon announced they were launching an operation in Brazil, we began thinking about getting our books translated into Portuguese, as well as other languages. It seemed that there was some potential out there for foreign editions in the common languages, such as German, Spanish and Portuguese.

If you are writing fiction, or general non-fiction, you may find this process easier than we did. The trouble with something as idiomatic as the guitar is that the translator must intimately understand the workings of the instrument to translate the text accurately. Even so, it was still fairly easy to find great translators who also played the guitar. We decided to start with German and found an incredible guitarist, ukulele player and translator named Elisabeth, who seemed perfect for the role. While other translators with no musical experience were tendering for work for $0.05 cents a word ($1,000 per book on average for us), Elisabeth was eager to work on an hourly basis and charge us $17 an hour.

The first book, including the cover text, product description and blurb was translated in around 14 hours and cost just $240. Since its publication, the translation of *The CAGED System and 100 Licks for Blues Guitar* (*Das CAGED System und 100 Licks für Blues-Gitarre*) has made over $10,000, representing a return on investment of over 4,000%. It took a few hours to find Elisabeth on Upwork and about an hour to publish the book once it was done.

When we could see that the translation was selling, we immediately put Elisabeth to work on other popular titles and got those to market as soon as we could. We were happy to increase her rate after she'd worked through a couple of books and she is still at work translating our back catalogue.

Our New Year's resolution in 2016 was to see all our books translated into Spanish and Portuguese, so in January we set about finding translators. We decided to go with South American variant Spanish and Portuguese, due to their larger populations and set about looking for translators on Upwork once again. We managed to find some translators who were also great guitarists.

The wanderlust of Joseph's youth finally paid off, because he has numbers of friends around the globe who are fluent in several languages. We asked the shortlist of translators to translate the same 500 words, then sent them to friends in far-off places. A few days later, they unanimously selected the same two translators for both Spanish and Portuguese languages.

We decided to use two translators for each language in order to get the job done quickly, but also as a failsafe method. In other words, they could check each other's work. Each translator worked on a different book then sent their work to the other to be proof read. When they were both happy we could go ahead and publish two translated titles that we had confidence in.

Of course, there were a few teething problems, but generally the system worked well and nine months later all of the books were translated into both Spanish and Portuguese, and about 15 books were finished in German. Instead of a total of 30 books in our list, we now had around 105.

The price was less than $14,000 for over 75 good quality translations. To put this into context, Fundamental Changes was earning around $2,000 a day in December 2016, so it was only 7-8 days' profit being reinvested into the business. If we had used a large translation agency it might have cost around $100,000 to get these books translated.

The average cost of hiring the translators was under $10 an hour. One of them was like a machine, reeling off full translations in under 10 hours at $8 an hour. In Brazil, with the currency crumbling and hyper-inflation, $10 an hour was an incredibly high wage, but our translator's fees were still substantially lower than the equivalent in Europe.

Fundamental Changes now owns those books as assets forever, as our contract with each translator stated that the job was a one-off piece of work, and that we would own the intellectual property of the translation. Everyone was happy with the arrangement.

The traditional model of translating a book involves a very complex, expensive process involving agents, translators, publishers, distributors, complicated rights licenses and lawyers. Everyone takes a cut.

Occasionally, if your book is very successful in English, you may be offered a "rights deal" whereby a company will take care of everything. Rights agencies will source reliable foreign language publishers, who will typically pay a small advance on royalties to secure the rights. The rights agent will take a percentage commission of all royalties for the lifetime of the book, and the foreign publisher will pay something like 15% of net revenue. Also, the publisher will own the resulting foreign edition.

In other words, though you won't have to do any work, the reward will be very small. By publishing your own foreign language editions you'll disrupt the translation industry and retain your intellectual property and international distribution rights – all in return for some upfront cash and setting up some interviews.

So how did it work out for us?

We won't lie. The Portuguese editions are slow burners. They tick along, but they're not setting the world alight. The Spanish and German editions are a completely different story. The prevalence of the Spanish language in the USA, combined with Amazon's excellent distribution of paperbacks to European countries, meant that these translations were in profit just a few months after the project was completed. In the six months that followed, translated paperbacks made around $12,000 and the Kindle editions just under $5,300 to give a total return of approximately $17,000 on the outlay of $14,000. The translations are still making around an extra $1,500 a month. That's a yearly return of 128% on the original investment with plenty of room for future growth.

The point here is that we leveraged work we'd already done, using freelancers to help us target new markets while retaining all the intellectual property rights. It is important that you see each of your books as an *asset* that should be working hard to make you money. Our input was minimal. We simply hired the freelancers and published the books.

If your work is selling well in English and you're interested in tapping new territories we suggest you start with German and Spanish translations. Take the time to employ the right translators and ensure their initial test submissions are excellent. Write a contract stating that all finished work belongs to you and that they don't have a right to an ongoing royalty. We also suggest signing a non-disclosure agreement if possible.

In summary, when you are able to, outsource! Don't carry the burden by yourself and make yourself stressed. Get the help you need and be wise in shopping around for the best people at the most competitive prices.

Chapter Sixteen: Publishing Other Authors

As musicians, we both have our strengths in certain musical genres, but there are many areas where we are weak. Other people will be able to write about and demonstrate those styles better than us. In 2014, as the Fundamental Changes brand was growing, it made sense to outsource some book writing to grow the company, and the decision was made to mine our own mailing list for musicians who could write the books we couldn't.

Joseph sent out an email asking for interested writers and from all the replies one in particular stood out. Simon joined the team in 2014 and has become a close friend. He is an excellent guitarist and has an amazing, good-natured stage presence. We asked him to make a few video lessons for our website to see how things developed. His work was excellent and he is also now in charge of our social media channels.

After a month or so of writing articles for the site Simon said he was ready to write his first book. The idea was excellent, so he was given the go-ahead and got working. A few months later, after a couple of false starts, we published the book and it sells a decent amount of copies each month.

This was the deal:

- Simon provided the manuscript of the book along with the notated examples and audio
- We provided the copyediting, proofreading, branding, covers, ISBNs, publishing, and promotion to our mailing list
- We split all the profits 50/50

We have continued to operate on a similar basis since, with varying splits of royalty revenue, depending on the context of the book and how it will be created. Occasionally we will commission musicians to write for us for a one-off fee, and sometimes it will be on a lower royalty rate, but everyone is always treated fairly and valued for their contribution.

This model has been a tremendous success. The brand has expanded and the authors (especially those who have written multiple books) have made a lot of money too.

On average, after Amazon have taken their cut, authors make around 25% of the cover price of a paperback book and 40% of a PDF edition. In mainstream publishing, the norm is 15% of *net revenue.* i.e. 15% of the money that is left after bookstore and distributor discounts, and sales commissions. That equates to about 7.5% of the cover price of a book in real terms.

As well as producing great content, we've also created some amazing opportunities for musicians to earn a living from what they do. It's difficult to make money as a creative person, as the route to success is often blocked by people with their hands in your pockets. It's a good feeling to be able to give something back to talented people.

Simon is currently writing his tenth book for Fundamental Changes and is an incredibly successful writer. It was years before he mentioned that he suffers from an autoimmune disease, is almost 100% housebound, and a part-time care giver for his mother. What he has achieved is nothing short of incredible and the fact that he never mentioned his challenges is a true testament to the wonderful person that he is.

Because Fundamental Changes has grown into a successful brand, we are regularly approached by people with ideas for a winning book. We consider many proposals and often uncover some real gems, but we work to one irrefutable principle: we won't cannibalise our own work. In other words, we don't release titles that will compete with the ones we've already published. That might sound quite limiting, but in practice it just makes us work very hard to find the unique selling point of any new project. Assuming a book is well-conceived and well-written, if it cannot be positioned to be distinct in our catalogue, we will we reluctantly turn it down.

We are currently working hard to find other instrumentalists who are interested in writing for our label with the goal of becoming the most prolific publisher of independent music books in the world.

We've said throughout this book that the long-term game plan should be to build a brand and build a fanbase – not just write one big masterpiece. As we've grown, we've been forced to think more like traditional publishers in respect to publishing other people efficiently and effectively. Publishers have, after all, been working to these principles for centuries for a reason.

Getting started with new authors

We hate legal stuff, but it is very important to set out what is expected from each party before entering into any type of publishing agreement. You're both going to have to deal with each other for a long time in the future, so it's best if you set things off on the right foot. We used a lawyer to create our initial publishing agreements. If you're going to publish someone else under your label, the process should look like this:

- Agree the book concept in broad terms
- Ask the person to write a chapter outline (you can download a model one from **http://geni.us/authordownloads**). Work with them to tweak this until it's in good shape
- Ask them to write a sample chapter. If it's a non-fiction book, get them to write a chapter where they are teaching something (not the introduction). You need to see how they handle their subject matter
- Once you have a sample chapter you're happy with, issue them a signed publishing agreement and wait to receive a countersigned copy back
- Agree a timeline for the project and set a target submission date (on which they will send in the finished manuscript)
- Agree the production timeline with the author (the time you'll need between the submission date and the target release date to carry out the production)

- Now let them get on with writing and check in periodically to see how they are doing (without micromanaging them). Offer support along the way if needed (such as feedback on chapters etc.)

If, for whatever reason, the project falls apart, you can agree rip up the contract and you've not lost too much. A bit of time, maybe, but you haven't ploughed hours of your time into editing/designing their book and you haven't spent any money. *C'est la vie.*

The best kind of publishing is relational, where it's both fun and productive. We aim to make friends with people before we publish them, and most of the people we publish (if we didn't know them beforehand) end up becoming our friends. If you're considering working with someone who has a great project, but your gut gives you a bad vibe about them, you probably shouldn't go ahead.

We treat our authors as partners, because the best, most successful publishing relationships are partnerships where each party brings their unique talents to the table. We respect our authors' input and opinions and, equally, we are committed to helping them grow as writers, so offer them our expertise in return.

Our goal is to make the publishing process as easy as possible, so we work closely with authors during the creative process. After five years and numerous bestselling books we've got a clear idea of what works and what doesn't in our genre. We both make ourselves available to authors any time for feedback, to answer questions or offer moral support and encouragement. Ultimately, this helps us get the book to market more quickly. Spending 20 minutes on Skype with an author is far easier than doing a rewrite later.

We also make our publishing "machine" available to our authors. They have access to the same transcribers and image editing team and they're encouraged to make full use of it. We would prefer to spend a few dollars on freelancers if it means our most valuable assets are producing great content quickly.

When books are submitted we work hard to bring them up to scratch and make them as excellent as every other book in our list. We give gracious, but direct and honest feedback, and if something is not working we'll have a conversation about it and find the right solution.

We both still have some books in us to write, but the next major phase of the company's life is about expansion, adding new authors to the roster, and commissioning books for different instruments. When you think about your own publishing plans, keep hold of the bigger vision of what could be, but stay committed to the detail and make sure that every book you put out is as exceptional as it can be.

Need some help?

If you don't want to perform every
publishing task yourself, we created,

www.self-published.co.uk

Professional services for every step
of the publishing process

Chapter Seventeen: Healthy Lifestyle, Money and The Future

A final word from Joseph:

In 2013–2014, despite living by the beach in Thailand I was working for around 18 hours a day writing, creating a brand, promoting my books and doing all the other little tasks that needed to be done to run a successful business. This amount of work wasn't healthy, but I thought I was building a resource that would allow me to retire early and scale back my efforts.

When I first moved to Thailand I was making around $13,000 a month in royalties and spending about $1,200 of that living very comfortably. Despite this apparent financial security, I found myself unfulfilled if I reduced my workload. Fundamental Changes had become my whole identity and I was incomplete unless it filled all my waking hours. While I had a lot of fun in Thailand and made some great friends, I regret not embracing some of the opportunities I was afforded there.

With my constant work, my girlfriend often warned me that I wasn't well and that I was burning out quickly. I ignored her and continued the same work regime when we moved back to Edinburgh a year later. At this point I was making close to $20,000 a month. I still identified strongly with my company and I reasoned to myself that it wasn't smart to step away from a business that was growing so quickly. I continued to take on more work and spent more time than ever at my desk.

Suddenly, and without warning, I broke.

I simply couldn't face going into the office in the morning and everything stopped for about a month. I refused to work, went outside, made some friends and enjoyed being in Edinburgh while I slowly recovered. I got well, my relationship improved and for the first time in a long while I was happy.

The big revelation came when I checked my sales figures and saw that they hadn't wavered in all the time I'd taken off. It slowly dawned on me that my business had become self-sufficient and if I wanted to step back slightly I could. It was weird to think that I'd managed to outsource myself from my own company and it was difficult to come to terms with.

I took another week off, just to check that my suspicions about my revenue were accurate and finally returned to work. This time I limited myself to four hours work a day, punctuated by breaks and exercise. I hit the gym hard and realised how weak I'd become. My whole body ached because of hours slumped over both my computer and my guitar. My muscles had atrophied and when I looked in the mirror I was shocked by what I saw.

As I said at the beginning of this book, money was never my motivation for writing. I truly enjoy helping people learn the guitar and it is an incredible feeling to know that so many people are learning music from my books.

However, over time I'd become fearful. I'd strived for years to gain security and I was terrified of it being taken away from me. I know from experience that I can live very well on a couple of thousand dollars a month, but for some reason I felt I needed to build a larger and larger buffer to protect my security, should everything collapse. Ironically, my need for security was the one thing making me most insecure.

It took me a long time to realise that it doesn't matter how much money you have if you kill yourself striving to achieve it.

If there's a lesson here it's about having balance in your life. Yes, there will be days when you will work 18 hours, but when you start to do well it's important to weigh up your work against the things that actually matter. The world goes past awfully quickly when you're watching it through an office window.

Life is about experiences, so go and grab them while you can. If you apply yourself to self-publishing and have any kind of talent for writing, it's not that hard to do what I've done. It just takes work, determination and attention to detail. Every major factor in my business has been discussed in detail in this book. Copy it and learn from my experience.

I do ask this of you, however. Look after yourself, take care of those around you and don't lock yourself away so that you come blinking out of your office in four years with a million dollars and no one to spend it with. A Christmas Carol springs to mind. Here are some practical health tips to help you enjoy the journey more than I have.

Stop every 15 or 20 minutes

Jump around for 3 minutes, spend a minute smiling into a mirror, say hello to someone. Regular breaks reduce the risk of burnout and your body will thank you for moving.

Exercise. Every day

Walk, run, join a gym, cycle, swim... exercise properly for an hour every day. Do some strength training to keep your back, neck and leg muscles supporting you while you work.

Get a standing desk

Sitting is just about the worst long-term thing you can do to your body apart from smoking. Standing desks can be made by putting your current desk on top of a plastic storage box. It doesn't have to cost a fortune and the health benefits are massive.

Drink water. Eat fruit

Have a jug of water nearby and a big bowl of fruit on your desk. You'll be surprised how much better you work when you're hydrated and full of vitamins. Don't snack on sweets or anything you know is bad. I'm English, so tea is obviously my vice, but I've learnt to stop drinking caffeine after 5.00pm and I sleep much better.

Have an office

Shut the door on your work at the end of the day and learn to leave your business brain in there too. You'll engage with real life a lot more quickly.

Stretch

Your body is an incredible machine that's designed to move. If you sit for long periods you'll get tight hips, lower back and hamstrings. Stretch thoroughly twice a day.

Get an accountant

When you make it big there's a lot of boring stuff you must do with numbers. My accountant makes sure that I see the bare minimum of this.

On having money...

I'm not a particularly extravagant person and I've never really been interested in clothes or fashion because I've been preoccupied with pursuits I found more meaningful. The best advice I ever got about spending money came from a friend who said, "Forget everything else, spend money on anything that comes between you and the floor."

This means that I've spent money on a nice mattress, decent shoes, good tyres and great underlay! (I've also got one of those fancy ultrasonic toothbrushes, so my dentist loves me). Boring I know, but all of these things protect my body. My one extravagance is that I see my strength and conditioning coach / boxing trainer every day. This may seem like a luxury, but investing in my health and fitness seems like a no-brainer to me.

The best thing about earning "a few quid" as we say in England is that I don't have any debt except for my mortgage. I was lucky enough to be able to save a 25% deposit for my house, so my repayments are very low. I bought my car second hand in cash, privately, and pay off my air miles credit card in full each month. My company maxes out my pension contributions each year, so I know I'm saving for the future. This, in turn, allows me to concentrate on the present.

While I'm not necessarily a big spender, I know that I don't have to worry about putting food on the table or going to a different country a few times a year. (Notice that I didn't use the word vacation! I always take a laptop and do some work sitting somewhere nice). In the middle of writing this book, a friend asked me to visit him in the Azores and I was on a plane the next day.

If anything, building up a bit of a cushion to guard against emergencies has allowed me to relax and engage more with life. I can be generous with friends, family and charities and share what I have when it's needed. I have a few friends who know how well my business is going. Sometimes they ask me why I continue to work. I think there are three reasons:

First, whenever I stop work for any period I feel my brain stagnating and I feel that I should be creating something new.

Second, I notice that my evening glass of wine starts to creep earlier and earlier.

Finally, the fear never completely goes away.

To be honest, I'd just like to get back to playing the guitar full time and I'm ready for the next big adventure.

The South of France looks nice…

Have fun.

Let's Get You Published!

We hope that you've enjoyed this book and have found it both informative and enlightening. To the uninitiated, the world of publishing can seem a baffling place, fraught with many pitfalls. In this book we've tried to demystify that world as much as possible and lay out a clear strategy for success.

We understand that everyone has different skills and different constraints on their time. For that reason there may be parts of the publishing process you relish being involved with, and other parts that don't fall within your skill set, or you simply haven't got time for. We're here to help.

Visit us at **www.self-published.co.uk** and you will find not only an informative blog with lots of publishing tips, but also a full range of services you can access. We offer authors an a la carte menu of services, so if you just want a cover designed, or a good editor, we can help. Alternatively, we can provide a full publishing package that includes every part of the process from start to finish.

See **https://www.self-published.co.uk/services/** for details.

Finally, we encourage you to make a start. Get writing! Make a decision to publish the idea that has been percolating for a long time. We wish you every success with your book.

Joseph & Tim

Twitter: **@spm_author**
Facebook: **https://www.facebook.com/groups/SPMauthor/**

Essential Resources & Friends of SPM

Community:

www.allianceindependentauthors.org
https://NonfictionAuthorsAssociation.com
https://NonfictionWritersConference.com

Writing/Publishing Resources:

www.betterbooktools.com/
www.upwork.com
www.grammarly.com
www.bowker.com
www.nielsen.com
www.ingramspark.com

Graphics Resources:

www.dafont.com
www.shutterstock.com
www.istockphoto.com
www.gettyimages.co.uk
www.canstockphoto.co.uk
www.pexels.com
www.stocksnap.io

Website Resources:

www.one.com/en/wordpress
www.lcn.com/web-hosting/wordpress
https://themeforest.net/category/wordpress

List Building:

https://mailchimp.com

www.activecampaign.com

www.bookbub.com

www.instafreebie.com

www.bookfunnel.com

www.readersintheknow.com/list-of-book-promotion-sites

Expert Self-Publishing Advice

https://selfpublishingformula.com

www.self-published.co.uk/services/

Self-published authors:

www.ljrossauthor.com

https://markjdawson.com

www.thecreativepenn.com

www.fundamental-changes.com

Printed in Great Britain
by Amazon